PERFECTING ME©

✦

BECOMING THE PERSON YOU WERE CREATED TO BE

✦

PER FECT ING ME ©

Compiled by
Dr. Wintley A. Phipps

WE ENCOURAGE YOU TO
TAKE THE
ONLINE ASSESSMENT.
URL: perfectingme.com

•

This companion study guide will
help you as you strive to reflect
God's character.

•

*"Only those who are perfect,
don't need perfecting."*

INTRODUCTION

Throughout the 17th and 18th centuries, Antonio Stradivari built the most extraordinary violins. The beauty and clarity of the sound are legendary. In 2010, centuries later, one of his violins sold for $16 million. As he labored in his studio, Stradivari had one rule: no violin was to leave the shop until it was as close to perfection as humanly possible. He is known to have said, "God needs violins to send His music into the world, and if my violins are defective, God's music will be spoiled."

I believe the lives we live are God's music to the world. In order for the music to be as beautiful as possible, our lives must be emptied of all that is unlike the character of God. Our lives must be in tune with the beauty of holiness.

If you are like me, you probably view becoming more like God and developing His character as both, exciting and daunting, noble and intimidating; a great dream, but impossible.

It has taken me many years to understand, to become a follower of Jesus means to live as He lived.

And no matter how overwhelming the thought, to accomplish that goal, I had to embrace the pursuit of Divine Perfection and the Character of God as my life's primary goal. I began to see the pursuit of Divine Perfection as fundamental to my character development and spiritual progress. And so "Perfecting Me" is all about the perfecting of our characters. It is not about; "Oh Perfect Me." It's about "God Perfecting Me!" I began to understand that my life is not my own. Jesus desires to live his life in me, in us, perfecting our characters.

I feel blessed to be able to say I have been in only one plane crash in my life, and more blessed because I am here to write about it. I was flying from Seattle to Spokane. As we came over the Cascade Mountains, it was dark and raining. Suddenly, we crashed on the tarmac. The pilot had forgotten to put down the wheels and landing gear! Thankfully, we all survived. This miracle is a constant reminder to me that in many cases we all really do want those who serve us to strive for perfection. It may be a physician who cares for our diseases, or the mechanic who has to assure that our cars are in tip-top shape. Or the athlete we pay money to watch on game day; or the teacher we count on to educate our children. We want those who serve us—especially the pilots who fly our planes, to strive for perfection. We don't want anything less from them than the pursuit of perfection, all day, every day, and in the case of pilots, every flight. Too much is at stake.

How is it then, that when it comes to serving God, we see the pursuit of perfection as optional? We see the pursuit of perfection as elective, something left entirely up to our discretion. We even believe we can cherry-pick where, how and when we want to put our best foot forward to resemble, reflect and reveal the character of God. We invite God to come into our lives and then tell Him what rooms are off limits. We tell Him what habits and attitudes we are serious about addressing and which ones we expect Him to overlook. Too often, this has crippled the advance and effectiveness of God's kingdom and has stained its witness. That is why we have professed followers of Jesus who fall anywhere it seems along the continuum of dysfunctional human behavior; from showing contempt to strangers, to holding a Bible in one hand and the chains of slaves in the other.

If there is anyone who knows that we are not perfect and cannot be perfect on our own, it is God Himself. Why then would He say to us, strive for perfection?

Matthew 5:48, Be ye therefore perfect, even as your Father which is in heaven is perfect.

Perhaps He knows that a part of our quest for transformation and restoration involves striving for perfection, even if on our own, we will never attain it. Too often our lives say to those around us, "we cannot attain perfection on our own, so don't bother trying!"

I ask if we are not striving for spiritual perfection, to what end are we striving? What are we seeking, and striving to attain every day?

Yes, none of us is perfect. Yet God has instructed us to pursue perfection. And we have grown so used to living with our imperfections, that to us, pursuing God's standard of perfection seems like reaching for the stars; possible—but highly unlikely.

Perhaps you've heard the name Vince Lombardi, the coach of the Green Bay Packers who, in a remarkable run, led his team to five NFL championships during the 1960s.

One day as he was motivating his team, Lombardi said these words: "Gentlemen, we will chase perfection, and we will chase it relentlessly, knowing all the while we can never attain it. But along the way, we shall catch excellence."

To be sure, "be ye therefore perfect" is more than a motivational pep talk on the football field of life. It is fundamental to living lives of blessing and victory. As we strive for perfection all day every day, we may not attain it, but we might just hit Christian maturity along the way.

Vince Lombardi

To say you know Jesus and love Him means you have committed yourself to the relentless pursuit of resembling and reflecting His character all day, every day. You commit to this life journey not when you feel like it, or when it is convenient, but all day every day. You commit to it not so you can earn heaven, but so you can do your best to live up to your highest calling and supreme destiny, to be; a reflection of His perfection.

As the moon reflects the light of the sun; each one of us was made to reflect the light of God's perfect character in our own. Remember it was Jesus Himself who said. "Be ye therefore perfect." He would never have said that to us if He didn't want us to try, and if He didn't know that in His power, we could succeed.

One writer said, "There are those who have known the pardoning love of Christ and who really desire to be children of God, yet they realize that their character is imperfect, their life faulty, and they are ready to doubt whether their hearts have been renewed by the Holy Spirit. To such I would say, Do not draw back in despair. We shall often have to bow down and weep at the feet of Jesus because of our shortcomings and mistakes, but we are not to be discouraged. Even if we are overcome by the enemy, we are not cast off, not forsaken and rejected of God. No; Christ is at the right hand of God, who also maketh intercession for us. Said the beloved John, "These things write I unto you, that ye sin not. And if any man sin, we have an advocate with the Father, Jesus Christ the righteous." *1 John 2:1*

And do not forget the words of Christ, "The Father Himself loveth you." John 16:27. He desires to restore you to Himself, to see His own purity and holiness reflected in you. And if you will but yield yourself to Him, He that hath begun a good work in you will carry it forward to the day of Jesus Christ. Pray more fervently; believe more fully. As we come to distrust our own power, let us trust the power of our Redeemer, and we shall praise Him who is the health of our countenance. SC 64

The closer you come to Jesus, the more faulty you will appear in your own eyes; for your vision will be clearer, and your imperfections will be seen in broad and distinct contrast to His perfect nature. This is evidence that Satan's delusions have lost their power; that the vivifying influence of the Spirit of God is arousing you. *SC.065.001*

No deep-seated love for Jesus can dwell in the heart that does not realize its own sinfulness. The soul that is transformed by the grace of Christ will admire His divine character; but if we do not see our own moral deformity, it is unmistakable evidence that we have not had a view of the beauty and excellence of Christ. *SC.065.002*

"But we all, with open face beholding as in a glass the glory of the Lord, are changed into the same image from glory to glory, even as by the Spirit of the Lord." The glory mentioned is character, and by faith we become changed from character to character. *ST.1893-04-17.011*

The less we see to esteem in ourselves, the more we shall see to esteem in the infinite purity and loveliness of our Savior. A view of our sinfulness drives us to Him who can pardon; and when the soul, realizing its helplessness, reaches out after Christ, He will reveal Himself in power. The more our sense of need drives us to Him and to the word of God, the more exalted views we shall have of His character, and the more fully we shall reflect His image. *SC.065.002*

Many years ago, in the 1950s, a pastor was traveling on a Greyhound bus. He was seated next to a college student who noticed when the pastor pulled out his Bible and began to read. When they came to a rough stretch in the road, the ride became extremely rough and bumpy. As the bus started to jostle them around, the pastor asked the young man "Are you ready for the temptations you will face in college?" The young man said to the Pastor, "I don't have a problem with temptation. I have strong willpower!" The minister quietly took a pencil out of his pocket and said, "Would you like to see me make this pencil stand up on the cover of this Bible even though our bus is going down a very bumpy road?" The young man said, "I'll believe it when I see it. I don't think you can do that." "See there," said the pastor "I'm doing it!" The young man laughed and said, "But you didn't tell me you would hold up the pencil with your hand." "I didn't have to tell you," the pastor said. "Have you ever seen a pencil stand up on its own without someone holding it?" The pastor then let go of the pencil. It shuddered and fell over. "The only reason you stand," the pastor said to the young man, "is because God is holding you up with His hand!" "If God were to remove His hand of protecting grace, you, like all of us, would immediately fall into sin." And so whatever perfection we attain along the way belongs to Jesus.

While God Himself uses the word 'perfection' liberally, with great hope and optimism, many today have even begun to see the word as offensive and odious. God has made Himself crystal clear on this point. He wants His people to strive for and seek perfection. Too many have all but shelved this instruction from God to be perfect. We've begun to treat the word perfection as if it were incompatible with modern-day Christian living. God has always found reasons to praise His faulty children while they were in pursuit of perfection.

Genesis 6:9 "These [are] the generations of Noah: Noah was a just man [and] perfect in his generations, [and] Noah walked with God." *Genesis 6:9 (NLT)*

"This is the account of Noah and his family. Noah was a righteous man, the only blameless person living on earth at the time, and he walked in close fellowship with God."

When God uses that word perfect, His idea of perfection is much more beautiful and substantive than we even realize. The Greek word used in the New Testament for perfection is the word "teleios" (pronounced tel-lee-os). In this case, the use of this Greek word means "one who has accomplished the intended goal." If something accomplishes what God designed it to do, God sees that as perfect. That's why in the eyes of God, even though a child is not fully grown; it is still perfect in the eyes of God. In God's kingdom, a bud is just as perfect as a rose in full bloom.

That word perfect or "teleios" or "telios" is also translated as "mature." When something grows to maturity, God sees it as being complete and perfect. To God, maturity and completeness are essential to perfection. In Genesis when God saw all He had made, it was complete, and God said, "Perfect."

Is the pursuit of perfection something we long for and pray for; that we might please God as we seek to measure up to the standard of perfection taught in His word?

Are we striving for perfection in our attitudes?

Are we striving for perfection in our thoughts and words?

The great artists Raphael, Michelangelo, and Leonardo da Vinci all had artistic perfection as their goal. The poets Dante and Milton, all had poetic perfection as their goal. The great composers Haydn, Handel, Beethoven, Bach, and Mendelssohn, all had musical perfection as their goal.

Noah's Ark

Don't you think that the perfecting of our characters should be an important goal of our spiritual lives?

Whenever we have failed to be a reflection of God's perfection, too often the results have been catastrophic. And when we fail, we should never lay the blame on God's lack of power. When we fail, we must lay the blame on our failure to ask for and appropriate the power God has made available to us. Our problem is because we know God has made provision for when we fail; we think the pursuit of perfection can be occasional and intermittent. Our pursuit of character perfection does not have to be sustained 24/7, all day, every day.

We believe because our mistakes are covered by the perfection of Christ; this exempts us from the pursuit of Christlikeness all day every day. We now think it convenient and less stressful to lower the bar in our quest to be restored in the image of God.

To be sure "none of us is perfect" and never will be perfect without the covering of His life. No matter how much we have accomplished or achieved, we will never have the luxury of looking at ourselves and saying "Perfect."

Anyone who claims to be perfect isn't, and in this life we shall never be faultless. Romans 12:3 (NLT)

[3] Because of the privilege and authority God has given me, I give each of you this warning: Don't think you are better than you really are. Be honest in your evaluation of yourselves, measuring yourselves by the faith God has given us.

In too many cases, however, we use this truism "Nobody's Perfect" to justify the imperfections we cherish. "Nobody's Perfect" is a truism. It is not a fait accompli. The truth is everybody increasingly can be more perfect every day and that is the doctrine Jesus taught. We are not perfect, but every day we strive to be.

In your attitudes, in your speech, in the use of your tongue and, you can strive to be perfect; all day every day. In your Christian life, you can choose to be relentless in your pursuit of perfection. In the choices you make, perfection can be your goal. You won't hit the mark every time, but what an exciting life you will lead—trying to live the way Jesus lived, all day; every day. Romans 6:13-18 (NLT)

[13] Do not let any part of your body become an instrument of evil to serve sin. Instead, give yourselves completely to God, for you were dead, but now you have new life. So use your whole body as an instrument to do what is right for the glory of God.

[14] Sin is no longer your master, for you no longer live under the requirements of

Michaelangelo

the law. Instead, you live under the freedom of God's grace.

¹⁵ Well then, since God's grace has set us free from the law, does that mean we can go on sinning? Of course not!

¹⁶ Don't you realize that you become the slave of whatever you choose to obey? You can be a slave to sin, which leads to death, or you can choose to obey God, which leads to righteous living.

¹⁷ Thank God! Once you were slaves of sin, but now you wholeheartedly obey this teaching we have given you.

¹⁸ Now you are free from your slavery to sin, and you have become slaves to righteous living.

We may not get it right every time or say it right every time, but what matters is that your goal is to be like Jesus. We will make mistakes. The question is: are we learning from our mistakes, or are we just content to repeat them? If we keep repeating the same mistakes, it is because we are not yet troubled enough by them to change. And only a commitment to the relentless pursuit of the perfection God has called us to, will motivate us to change.

Now there are those who say, "We cannot be perfect. So don't even try! Don't put so much pressure on yourself." But that's not what God says. Nowhere in the Bible have I seen a scripture that says: "You're not perfect, so go easy on yourself." And anytime we deliberately choose to ease up on our pursuit of Christlike perfection, we diminish our humanity and endanger our very souls' salvation. We reject the very power God gives us to be like Jesus. Today, God wants you to reject that; "Stop trying to be perfect" teaching.

There is no other area of life, either scientific or professional, where we should or would accept this;

"We can't be perfect, so stop trying" thinking. Try that on your job; and see how far that will get you. Try that in college or in your marriage and see how far that will get you. And neither should we accept it in our personal lives. The moment we accept the pursuit of anything less than perfection, we degrade our humanity and devalue all God has called us to be, a reflection of His perfection.

Today I invite you to accept with joy and enthusiasm, God's challenge to strive to be perfect; all day every day. Embrace God's call to strive to be more every day what you understand His perfection to be.

Resembling, Reflecting and Revealing His character is God's will for our lives.

There is one more important thing to remember. In our own pursuit of perfection, we must be careful that we only apply our standards of perfection to ourselves—NOT to others! The moment we do, we will become judgmental. God made our eyes to see outward; and not inward. As a result we see the faults of others much more easily than we see our own. Jesus knew this would be the tendency of our sinful human nature.

That's why He taught us in Matthew 7:

Matthew 7:1 "Judge not, that ye be not judged. Apply your understanding of perfection to yourself and not to others."

Matthew 7:2 "For with what judgment ye judge, ye shall be judged: and with what measure ye mete, it shall be measured to you again."

Matthew 7:3 "And why beholdest thou the mote that is in thy brother's eye, but considerest not the beam that is in thine own eye?"

Matthew 7:4 "or how wilt thou say to thy brother, let me pull out the mote out of thine eye; and, behold, a beam [is] in thine own eye?"

Matthew 7:5 "Thou hypocrite, first cast out the beam out of thine own eye; and then shalt thou see clearly to cast out the mote out of thy brother's eye."

Matthew 7:3 (NLT) "Why are you so picky with your brother when you probably have bigger faults than he has?"

Matthew 7:4 "How do you expect to help him when you can't even see your own mistakes?"

Matthew 7:5 "What you need is to correct your own faults first; then you'll be better able to discern what is wrong with others.

Ultimately the pursuit of perfection can only be a personal decision, and one you apply to your own life. We can try to inspire and motivate others but ultimately we should apply those expectations to our own lives.

There is a reason throughout the corporate world you will often see the term "Zero Defects" on the floors of assembly lines, on signs, posters, and employee badges. The reason is this: the cost of one defect can be far too high. Ask General Motors, ask Wall Street! That's why presidents and supervisors, managers and administrators, are trying to inspire workers to take pride in what they do and to aim for perfection. all day, every day.

I believe God does not expect perfection from us every day. He already knows we are going to make mistakes. But God does expect the pursuit of perfection; all day, every day.

God expects us every day to grow more and more into Christian maturity. We are challenged by God today to be perfect, to be reflections of His perfection; to be perfect reproductions of His character.

I tell people all the time, if you find a perfect church, don't join it—you will spoil it! But churches that are growing and producing people who live and look more like Jesus are needed now more than ever.

Dante Alighieri

Beethoven

A Christlike or Christ like life is the most powerful argument that can be advanced in favor of Christianity, and a cheap Christian character works more harm in the world than the character of a worldly people. Not all the books written can serve the purpose of a holy life. Men will believe, not what the minister preaches, but what the church lives. Too often the influence of the sermon preached from the pulpit is counteracted by the sermon preached in the lives of those who claim to be advocates of truth. *9T.021.002*

It is the purpose of God to glorify Himself in His people before the world. He expects those who bear the name of Christ to represent Him in thought, word, and deed. Their thoughts are to be pure and their words noble and uplifting, drawing those around them nearer the Savior. The religion of Christ is to be interwoven with all that they do and say. Their every business transaction is to be fragrant with the presence of God. *9T.021.003*

The life that Christ lived in this world, men and women can live through His power and under His instruction. In their conflict with Satan they may have all the help that He had. They may be more than conquerors through Him who loved them and gave Himself for them. *9T.022.002*

The lives of professing Christians who do not live the Christ life are a mockery to religion. Everyone whose name is registered on the church roll is under obligation to represent Christ by revealing the inward adorning of a meek and quiet spirit. They are to be his witnesses, making known the advantages of walking and working as Christ has given them example. The truth for this time is to appear in its power in the lives of those who believe it, and is to be imparted to the world. Believers are to represent in their lives its power to sanctify and ennoble. *9T.022.003*

The inhabitants of the heavenly universe expect the followers of Christ to shine as lights in the world. They are to show forth the power of the grace that Christ died to give men. God expects those who profess to be Christians to reveal in their lives the highest development of Christianity. They are recognized representatives of Christ, and they are to show that Christianity is a reality. They are to be men of faith, men of courage, whole-souled men, who, without questioning, trust in God and his promises. *9T.023.001*

The eight areas of spiritual development we focus on in this study guide are not meant to be exhaustive, clinical or comprehensive. They are meant to be a step forward towards a framework for personal spiritual development. It is an effort to embrace the work God has begun in our lives and will see to completion, the work of "Perfecting Me." Every day, as you cooperate with God, He is perfecting you.

Every day, "we are to add to faith, virtue; and to virtue, knowledge; and to knowledge, temperance; and to temperance, patience; and to patience, godliness; and to godliness, brotherly kindness; and to brotherly kindness, charity. You are not to think that you must wait until you have perfected one grace, before cultivating another. No; they are to grow up together, fed continually from the fountain of charity; every day that you live, you can be perfecting the blessed attributes fully revealed in the character of Christ; and when you do this, you will bring light, love, peace, and joy into your homes. *RH.1890-12-09.004*

My prayer is that this study guide will help you grow every day to more Resemble Reflect and Reveal the Character of Christ.

TABLE OF CONTENTS

CHAPTER 1
FAITH AND BELIEF

You know you're about to do something bordering on the edge of insanity when the Red Bull stimulant drink company offers to sponsor you.

Felix Baumgartner didn't come from a family of daredevils. Neither his brother, a chef, nor his parents would have ever jumped off Rio de Janeiro's 130-foot Christ the Redeemer Statue, much less Kuala Lumpur's 1,483-foot Petronas Towers as Felix did. But for Felix, the Austrian daredevil, the thrills those heights offered just weren't enough.

Then came the idea.

The idea germinated into faith and belief that was so contagious it attracted a 300-member team of scientists, engineers, and physicians—and, of course, the attention of Red Bull Stratos. Felix Baumgartner was attempting to shatter world records with a 24-mile freefall, but beyond that, he was going to try to break the sound barrier—with his own body.

During his training, Baumgartner experienced panic attacks—not from the fear of heights or falling, but from claustrophobia, after being trapped inside his space suit for long hours. It was a psychological and physiological response to fear that almost defeated the entire project until Baumgartner faced his terror with the help of a psychologist and was able to manage it enough to continue.

There were other fears that were well-founded.

The worst thing that could happen to Baumgartner, he knew, would be for him to go into an uncontrollable spin. At that point, the centrifugal force would push his blood from the center of his body. Baumgartner knew that if that happened, the only way for blood to leave his body would be through his eyeballs. After he had completed his fall, Felix reminisced about all that could have gone wrong: "That means you're dead," Felix said. "That was what we feared most."

Felix Baumgartner

Eight million people hovered around their computer screens on October 14, 2012 to watch YouTube live video streaming of Baumgartner's four-minute, 20-second free fall from space.

Guided by the calming voice of 84-year old Joe Kittinger, the man whose record Baumgartner intended to break, Felix ascended in a capsule suspended from a balloon into the black edge of space.

Just before he plunged into the emptiness beneath him in only his spacesuit, he said, "I know the whole world is watching, and I wish the whole world could see what I see. Sometimes you have to go up really high to understand how small you really are."

The world held its breath as Baumgartner leaped from his capsule and became a tiny, blurry white dot against a vast backdrop of black nothingness. Moments later, he found himself caught in the dreaded spin, and millions of people looked on, wondering if they were about to witness a tragic ending to Baumgartner's brave attempt.

To everyone's relief, he was able to recover. Before safely landing in New Mexico less than four and a half minutes later, Baumgartner's body reached Mach 1.24 at 833.9 miles per hour, which is faster than the speed of sound.

That's what happens when a person believes.

The power to believe is a character trait that is ethically neutral. It can be used, in the immortal words of Obi Wan Kenobi in Star Wars, for good or evil. It is one of the most important and far-reaching faculties a person has. The power to believe and the ability to choose what we believe, shapes our lives, circumstances, character, behavior, and destiny more than any other single factor.

Training yourself to believe requires 1) listening and responding to the sense of destiny you feel inside, and 2) not allowing negative thoughts and insecurities to smother that sense of destiny. Both of those requirements are choices—which means they are within your power to do them.

What is the faith and belief that propels you toward your destiny?

Your grandparents might tell you it is faith and belief in the American dream.

Your college professor—and, ironically, most reality television stars—might tell you it is faith and belief in yourself.

A recovering alcoholic struggling to rebuild his life will tell you it is faith and belief in a higher power.

From my own personal experience, I will tell you it is faith and belief in God.

It's easy to believe in what you can see and touch and hear. But to push yourself beyond what is obvious to everyone and believe in what you cannot—at least initially—grasp in your two hands, that's when true faith and belief is born. That's when you can reach beyond your present circumstances and achieve more than you know to be possible. Without the ability to believe, we would be nothing more than complicated organisms. We would never search for higher life or try to do anything outside the realm of existing. We would fail to appreciate what is magnificent. Our lives would have no majesty and no meaning.

In the psycho-economy of man, believing is the currency that changes everything. No matter how irrational it may seem, believing has the power to alter our circumstances and rearrange our destinies. Faith and belief have proven throughout history to have the power to motivate the human heart.

To believe is to outgrow our fear of not living up to our potential. For some, ironically, it's outgrowing the fear of living up to our potential. Believing pushes us to search and dream and do.

So how does it work?

If you've seen the movie First Knight, you will remember the heart-stopping scene when Lancelot realizes he can earn a kiss from queen-to-be Guinevere if he runs the gauntlet and survives. Without any armor or padding, Lancelot shocks everyone by instinctively making his way through the swinging blades and crushing weights to get to the other side. One wrong move and he would be pulp. (I won't tell you what happens, in case you haven't seen it.)

That's an analogy for the route an idea takes to become faith and belief.

The idea presents itself but must survive the filters we have in our minds—filters like culture, rationality, and sensibility. Filters like prior knowledge, personal judgment, and preferences, in addition to personal experience and what we already know to be true. If the idea survives the deadly swinging axes of our thought processes, it is offered up for consideration to our will, which then decides whether or not to embrace it as our new faith and belief. At that point, we make a choice, and the idea becomes a new belief.

Have you ever noticed that when someone embraces a faith or belief, it's very difficult to change it or destroy it? They will defend that faith and belief fiercely and loyally. Believing is so powerful it can bend and alter our perceptions of reality.

Be careful what you believe, because faith and belief become powerful magnets that draw people, resources, and destiny to your door. They change the course of your life.

If you believe you can't you won't. If you believe you can't succeed you don't.

When what you believe is stronger than what seems inevitable, then that faith and belief becomes sacred. Its powers of persuasion motivate you to consider possibilities others haven't dreamed of, and enable you to harness conviction and confidence. You are inspired by what you believe is possible.

You may not be trying to break world records, but you are called to believe outside yourself. And that faith and belief will move you to action because faith and belief are power.

According to French Philosopher Voltaire (and Peter Parker's Uncle Ben in the movie Spider-man), "With great power comes great responsibility." When it comes to using the power of faith and belief, that means your faith and belief must be guided by an internal compass.

Read through these scriptures

Hebrews 11:6 "But without faith [it is] impossible to please [him]: for he that cometh to God must believe that he is, and [that] He is a rewarder of them that diligently seek Him."

Romans 1:17 "For therein is the righteousness of God revealed from faith to faith: as it is written, The just shall live by faith."

Romans 5:1 "Therefore being justified by faith, we have peace with God through our Lord Jesus Christ:"

Romans 5:2 "By whom also we have access by faith into this grace wherein we stand, and rejoice in hope of the glory of God."

Galatians 5:5 "For we through the Spirit wait for the hope of righteousness by faith."

2 Corinthians 5:7 "(For we walk by faith, not by sight:)"

Galatians 2:20 "I am crucified with Christ: nevertheless I live; yet not I, but Christ liveth in me: and the life which I now live in the flesh I live by the faith of the Son of God, who loved me, and gave himself for me."

Ephesians 2:8 "For by grace are ye saved through faith; and that not of yourselves: [it is] the gift of God."

Ephesians 3:16 "That he would grant you, according to the riches of his glory, to be strengthened with might by his Spirit in the inner man."

Ephesians 3:17 "That Christ may dwell in your hearts by faith; that ye, being rooted and grounded in love..."

Ephesians 6:16 "Above all, taking the shield of faith, wherewith ye shall be able to quench all the fiery darts of the wicked."

Hebrews 10:38 "Now the just shall live by faith: but if [any man] draw back, my soul shall have no pleasure in him."

James 2:17 "Even so faith, if it hath not works, is dead, being alone."

James 2:18 "Yea, a man may say, Thou hast faith, and I have works: show me thy faith without thy works, and I will show thee my faith by my works."

James 2:23 "And the scripture was fulfilled which saith, Abraham believed God, and it was imputed unto him for righteousness: and he was called the Friend of God."

James 2:24 "Ye see then how that by works a man is justified, and not by faith only."

James 2:26 "For as the body without the spirit is dead, so faith without works is dead also."

1 John 5:4 "For whatsoever is born of God overcometh the world: and this is the victory that overcometh the world, [even] our faith."

Think through and check the box that fits what you think

1. Faith is fundamental to building character that resembles the character of God.

1) ☐ strongly agree   2) ☐ agree   3) ☐ neutral   4) ☐ disagree   5) ☐ strongly disagree

2. By dwelling upon the love of God and our Saviour, by contemplating the perfection of the divine character and claiming the righteousness of Christ as ours by faith, we are to be transformed into the same image.

1) ☐ strongly agree   2) ☐ agree   3) ☐ neutral   4) ☐ disagree   5) ☐ strongly disagree

3. We must have faith in Christ if we would reflect the divine character.

1) ☐ strongly agree   2) ☐ agree   3) ☐ neutral   4) ☐ disagree   5) ☐ strongly disagree

4. There can be no perfection of Christian character without that faith that works by love, and purifies the soul.

1) ☐ strongly agree   2) ☐ agree   3) ☐ neutral   4) ☐ disagree   5) ☐ strongly disagree

5. Faith in Jesus Christ as your personal Saviour, will give strength and solidity to your character.

1) ☐ strongly agree   2) ☐ agree   3) ☐ neutral   4) ☐ disagree   5) ☐ strongly disagree

6. It is the righteousness of Christ, His own unblemished character that through faith is imparted to all who receive Him as their personal Saviour.

1) ☐ strongly agree   2) ☐ agree   3) ☐ neutral   4) ☐ disagree   5) ☐ strongly disagree

7. All are lost through Adam. Our only hope is a transformation of character through repentance and faith in Christ as our personal Saviour.

1) ☐ strongly agree   2) ☐ agree   3) ☐ neutral   4) ☐ disagree   5) ☐ strongly disagree

8. Faith will sustain works, for faith works by love and purifies the soul.

1) ☐ strongly agree   2) ☐ agree   3) ☐ neutral   4) ☐ disagree   5) ☐ strongly disagree

Highlight thoughts below that expresses what you believe

Through the merits of Christ, through His righteousness, which by faith is imputed unto us, we are to attain to the perfection of Christian character. *5T.744.002*

Faith in Christ as the world's Redeemer calls for an acknowledgment of the enlightened intellect controlled by a heart that can discern and appreciate the heavenly treasure. This faith is inseparable from repentance and transformation of character. To have faith means to find and accept the gospel treasure, with all the obligations which it imposes. *COL.112.005*

Faith in Christ as the world's Redeemer calls for an acknowledgment of the enlightened intellect controlled by a heart that can discern and appreciate the heavenly treasure. This faith is inseparable from repentance and transformation of character. To have faith means to find and accept the gospel treasure, with all the obligations which it imposes. *COL.112.005*

It is the righteousness of Christ, His own unblemished character, that through faith is imparted to all who receive Him as their personal Saviour. *COL.310.004*

It is the privilege of every soul to reach the highest standard. Stop at no low standard in your experience. Beware of admitting any worldly or selfish motives whatever in the settlement of the great question between God and your soul. The Lord requires all that there is of you through constant improvement of every talent, that you may make a success in the formation of Christian character. By faith let the Holy Spirit instruct you, that you may not only receive but impart the heavenly grace. *GH.1899-12-01.002*

It is not by looking away from him that we imitate the life of Jesus, but by talking of him, by dwelling upon his perfections, by seeking to refine the taste and elevate the character, by trying, through faith and love, and by earnest, persevering effort, to approach the perfect Pattern. By having a knowledge of Christ,--his words, his habits, and his lessons of instruction,--we borrow the virtues of the character we have so closely studied, and become imbued with the spirit we have so much admired. Jesus becomes to us "the chiefest among ten thousand," the One "altogether lovely". *RH.1887-03-15.013*

Jesus said unto them, I am the bread of life: he that cometh to me shall never hunger; and he that believeth on me shall never thirst."

From these words you may understand the character of real faith in Christ; it is a faith that lays hold upon his divine merits. It is the faith spoken of as "the substance of things hoped for, the evidence of things not seen." *RH.1891-04-14.004*

The eye of faith sees him ever present, in all his goodness, grace forbearance, courtesy, and love, those spiritual and divine attributes. And as we behold, we are changed into his likeness. *RH.1891-04-28.007*

To those who have obtained the faith that filled the hearts of Christians in Peter's time, are written the words: "Grace and peace be multiplied unto you through the knowledge of God, and of Jesus our Lord." In the light of this instruction, how important it is that we give strict attention to the formation of character! He who by faith daily lays hold firmly upon the invisible One, will reveal the character of Jesus. With lowliness of heart he will accept Christ's invitation to the weary and the heavy laden. Instead of unloading his burdens upon his neighbor, with whose heart-sorrows and burdens he is unacquainted, he will seek rest by taking upon himself the yoke of Christ. Let us abide in Jesus. Then he alone--formed within, the hope of glory--will appear in our every word and deed. *RH.1904-05-26.003*

Faith is made perfect by works. Those who make no change in character, though claiming the privilege of being called Christians, have not on the wedding garment. *RH.1900-05-08.018*

The end of our faith is the perfection of human character, the sanctification of the entire being *RH.1901-10-01.011*

Those who claim that faith alone will save them, are trusting to a rope of sand; for faith is made perfect by good works. *RH.1911-04-13.015*

True faith takes the word of God and weaves it into the life and character. *ST.1888-07-27.003*

By beholding Christ he will learn to hate sin that has brought to his Redeemer suffering and death. By beholding, his faith is made strong, and he comes to know "the only true God, and Jesus Christ, whom Thou hast sent." The sinner sees Jesus as he is, full of compassion and tender love, and by beholding the manifestation of his great love toward fallen man in his sufferings of Calvary, he is transformed in character. *ST.1894-02-12.002*

If we follow on to know the Lord, we shall know that his goings forth are prepared as the morning. He is perfecting Christian character after the divine model, is growing in faith, in influence and power, and this work will progress in his character until faith is lost in sight, and grace in glory. The righteousness of Christ is imputed to the obedient soul, and the peace of Christ is an abiding principle in the heart. *ST.1895-05-16.006*

Faith is inseparable from repentance and transformation of character. *ST.1899-01-18.015*

"Without faith it is impossible to please him." And "whatsoever is not of faith is sin."[HEB. 11:6; ROM. 14:23.] *GC88.436.001*

Feeling is no criterion for any of us. "Faith is the substance of things hoped for, the evidence of things not seen."[HEB. 11:1.] We are to examine our character in God's mirror, his holy law, to detect our errors and imperfections, and then to remove them by the precious blood of Christ. *GW92.427.003*

CHAPTER 2
VIRTUE

She promised him her parents wouldn't be home when he showed up.

In the chat room, they had already talked about what they would do when he arrived, and had exchanged pictures. She was a shy but curious 14-year-old, and he was a married 38-year-old real estate agent and father, looking forward to showing her how to please a man. That evening, he arrived at her house, never suspecting that Chris Hanson and a Dateline NBC television film crew for the show "To Catch a Predator"—as well as a team of police officers—were waiting for him. It was a sting operation, and he was caught.

In another part of the country, a woman sits in a nail salon receiving a pedicure and talking on her phone to a friend, using racial slurs and making fun of the Asian nail technician—whom the woman assumes speaks no English—in front of the other shocked salon patrons. While the "racist" woman is an actor, the other patrons don't know this. Faced with a situation that makes them uncomfortable, they individually decide whether to ignore what is happening, or intervene. Again, hidden cameras capture the entire event—this time, for the ABC show called "What Would You Do?"

It's been said that your character is who you are when no one is watching—or, in the cases above, who you are when you think no one is watching.

Virtue is the fence inside all of us that separates appropriate desires from inappropriate desires. Unfortunately, for some people, that fence is only for looks—like a white picket fence, it has the outward appearance of virtue, though it doesn't serve its purpose. For others, that dimension of character is so well developed and trustworthy, it might as well be a 12-foot fence topped with razor wire. Solid. Safe. Trustworthy.

Virtue is not valued in much of society today. Many people believe in doing whatever they need to do to get ahead, and if someone else suffers in the process, so be it.

That makes virtue especially important for two reasons: 1) it is a lost art, the absence of which strips integrity and beauty from the face of society, and 2) it is a significant dimension that cannot be neglected in the development of a fully functioning character.

Virtue has to be developed and maintained, because it will be tested in every aspect of your life—even in your own mind.

Your mind has an incredible ability to justify your behavior. "Just this once." "This isn't hurting anyone." "Other people have done a lot worse." The list of excuses is endless—and every excuse acts as dead weight on your climb to greatness.

It's very difficult to spend time around virtue without developing some for yourself. That's why it's important to surround yourself with people who have character choose character-supporting entertainment and continue practicing virtue so you influence others.

How do you practice virtue?

• Be the boss of your thoughts. Thoughts precede actions, actions become habits, and habits become character. If you find your thoughts wandering into immoral territory, take them back and focus on what's true and moral.

• Let everything around you pass through your "virtue" filter. Process what you see and hear and determine whether to accept it as part of who you are or not.

• Prepare for attack on your virtue. There will always be a situation, a person, a feeling that challenges the character you are building. Those are opportunities to strengthen who you are becoming. Fight against the temptation to give in to destructive behavior.

If you've watched reality TV lately, you've probably noticed that the character trait most reality stars seem to be working hard to maintain is selfishness. From housewives who have nothing better to do than think about themselves and their hurt feelings, to "sweet" sixteen-year-olds who expect the world to revolve around them; to youth who confuse self-destructive behavior with "finding" and "differentiating" themselves.

Virtue, on the other hand, is a powerful gift. Your sense of virtue (also called your "conscience") is always there, guiding you to use good judgment. Your sense of virtue helps you choose activities that are worthy of your time and effort. Your sense of virtue, inborn but so often corrupted, provides the only way to be the best you can be. In short, your virtue is what preserves your humanity; it is one of the greatest checks you have against destructive behavior.

Believing may be the first step toward the development of human character. But belief falters without virtue. Like every other human being, you were born with the capacity for virtue, and choosing a life of purity of thought and action is a badge of honor in terms of your humanity.

So much of the best in you depends upon the constant protection of your thoughts and behaviors. What consumes your thoughts consumes you! If you allow foul and contaminated thoughts to overtake your mind, you end up living in a soiled and degraded atmosphere.

Just as with belief, virtue requires a full commitment.

If we are to be among the greats, the heroes, if we are going to build character that is ready for moments of destiny, we can't sacrifice virtue in any aspect of our lives.

If there is a habit that is keeping you locked in immorality, put virtue in control. Do it now. Take charge of your life, your thoughts, your actions, and your destiny.

Virtue has benefits for your life. The scriptures and questions below will help you determine your level of virtue development, as well as measure whether or not you are reaping the benefits of virtue.

Philippians 4:8 "Finally, brethren, whatsoever things are true, whatsoever things [are] honest, whatsoever things [are] just, whatsoever things [are] pure, whatsoever things [are] lovely, whatsoever things [are] of good report; if [there be] any virtue, and if [there be] any praise, think on these things."

Read through these scriptures

2 Peter 1:3 "According as his divine power hath given unto us all things that [pertain] unto life and godliness, through the knowledge of him that hath called us to glory and virtue:"

2 Peter 11:4 "Whereby are given unto us exceeding great and precious promises: that by these ye might be partakers of the divine nature, having escaped the corruption that is in the world through lust."

2 Peter 11:5 "And beside this, giving all diligence, add to your faith virtue;"

Psalms 7:10 "My defence [is] of God, which saveth the upright in heart."

Psalms 11:7 "For the righteous LORD loveth righteousness; his countenance doth behold the upright."

Psalms 18:25 "With the merciful thou wilt show thyself merciful; with an upright man thou wilt show thyself upright;"

Psalms 19:13 "Keep back thy servant also from presumptuous [sins]; let them not have dominion over me: then shall I be upright, and I shall be innocent from the great transgression."

Psalms 25:20 "O keep my soul, and deliver me: let me not be ashamed; for I put my trust in thee."

Psalms 25:21 "Let integrity and uprightness preserve me; for I wait on thee."

Psalms 26:11 "But as for me, I will walk in mine integrity: redeem me, and be merciful unto me."

Psalms 32:11 "Be glad in the LORD, and rejoice, ye righteous: and shout for joy, all [ye that are] upright in heart."

Psalms 33:1 "Rejoice in the LORD, O ye righteous: [for] praise is comely for the upright."

Psalms 36:10 "O continue thy lovingkindness unto them that know thee; and thy righteousness to the upright in heart."

Psalms 37:18 "The LORD knoweth the days of the upright: and their inheritance shall be forever."

Psalms 37:37 "Mark the perfect [man], and behold the upright: for the end of [that] man [is] peace."

Proverbs 11:3 "The integrity of the upright shall guide them:"

Proverbs 11:20 "They that are of a forward heart [are] abomination to the LORD: but [such as are] upright in [their] way [are] His delight."

Proverbs 14:2 "He that walketh in his uprightness feareth the LORD: but [he that is] perverse in his ways despiseth him."

Proverbs 15:8 "The sacrifice of the wicked [is] an abomination to the LORD: but the prayer of the upright [is] his delight."

Proverbs 19:1 "Better [is] the poor that walketh in his integrity, than [he that is] perverse in his lips, and is a fool."

Proverbs 20:7 "The just [man] walketh in his integrity: his children [are] blessed after him."

Proverbs 28:6 "Better [is] the poor that walketh in his uprightness, than [he that is] perverse [in his] ways, though he [be] rich."

Isaiah 26:7 "The way of the just [is] uprightness: thou, most upright, dost weigh the path of the just."

Think through and check the box that fits what you think

1. Faith without virtue will destroy you.

1) ☐ strongly agree   2) ☐ agree   3) ☐ neutral   4) ☐ disagree   5) ☐ strongly disagree

2. All that defiles, corrupts and contaminates character must be quarantined and deleted from the mind and life.

1) ☐ strongly agree   2) ☐ agree   3) ☐ neutral   4) ☐ disagree   5) ☐ strongly disagree

3. Proverbs 14: 34 Godliness makes a nation great, but sin is a disgrace to any people.

1) ☐ strongly agree   2) ☐ agree   3) ☐ neutral   4) ☐ disagree   5) ☐ strongly disagree

4. Virtue gives us the power to stand against temptation.

1) ☐ strongly agree   2) ☐ agree   3) ☐ neutral   4) ☐ disagree   5) ☐ strongly disagree

5. Virtue cleanses the heart and prepares the mind to welcome the beauty of the perfect character of God.

1) ☐ strongly agree   2) ☐ agree   3) ☐ neutral   4) ☐ disagree   5) ☐ strongly disagree

6. A character of integrity and virtue, represents the Character of Jesus.

1) ☐ strongly agree   2) ☐ agree   3) ☐ neutral   4) ☐ disagree   5) ☐ strongly disagree

7. We must constantly be developing in Character in true virtue and godliness.

1) ☐ strongly agree   2) ☐ agree   3) ☐ neutral   4) ☐ disagree   5) ☐ strongly disagree

8. Every passing year should increase the soul's yearning for purity and perfection of Christian character.

1) ☐ strongly agree   2) ☐ agree   3) ☐ neutral   4) ☐ disagree   5) ☐ strongly disagree

Highlight thoughts below that expresses what you believe

Having received the faith of the gospel, the next work of the believer is to add to his character virtue, Faith is the first round in the ladder of advancement. Without faith it is impossible to please God. But many stop on this round, and never ascend higher. They seem to think that when they have professed Christ, when their names are on the church record, their work is completed. Faith is essential; but the inspired word says, "Add to your faith, virtue." Those who are seeking for eternal life, and a home in the kingdom of God, must lay for their character building the foundation of virtue. Jesus must be the chief corner stone. The things that defile the soul must be banished from the mind and life. When temptations are presented, they must be resisted in the strength of Christ. The virtue of the spotless Lamb of God must be woven into the character till the soul can stand in its integrity. "Submit yourselves therefore to God. Resist the Devil, and he will flee from you." *RH.1888-02-21.004*

We are to keep Christ as our pattern ever in view, and by contemplating him we become transformed in character. His own righteousness is imputed to us. Therefore all virtue, all light, all that is of any value, is derived from Christ; and how foolish for any man to cherish self-esteem, and lift up his soul unto vanity. Christ is everything to us, and if we have his love abiding in our hearts, we shall cultivate love for one another. *MM.1893-10-01.005*

Faith is essential; but the inspired word says, "Add to your faith, virtue." Those who are seeking for eternal life, and a home in the kingdom of God, must lay for their character building the foundation of virtue. Jesus must be the chief corner stone. The things that defile the soul must be banished from the mind and life. When temptations are presented, they must be resisted in the strength of Christ. The virtue of the spotless Lamb of God must be woven into the character till the soul can stand in its integrity. "Submit yourselves therefore to God. Resist the Devil, and he will flee from you." *RH.1888-02-21.004*

In his dealing with men, God has often demonstrated that through the virtue obtained by obedience to the laws of heaven, human beings may gain a beauty of character that will fit them to be laborers together with him.

Purity of character will be distinctly revealed by all who truly follow Christ. *RH.1905-08-31.006*

Believers and "workers for God must live as in his sight, and be constantly developing in character, true virtue, and godliness. Their minds and hearts must be so thoroughly imbued with the spirit of Christ, and solemnized by the sacred message they have to bear, that every thought, every action, and every motive will be above the earthly and sensual. Their happiness will not be in forbidden, selfish gratification, but in Jesus and his love." *ST.1885-10-15.008*

Having received the faith of the gospel, the next work of the believer is to add to his character virtue, and thus cleanse the heart and prepare the mind for the reception of the knowledge of God. This knowledge is the foundation of all true education and of all true service. It is the only real safeguard against temptation; and it is this alone that can make one like God in character. Through the knowledge of God and of His Son Jesus Christ, are given to the believer "all things that pertain unto life and godliness." No good gift is withheld from him who sincerely desires to obtain the righteousness of God. *AA.531.001*

CHAPTER 3

KNOWLEDGE

Smart people know the facts.

Wise people know how to use the facts to their advantage.

When William Lamar "Billy" Beane III began managing the Oakland Athletics baseball team, the franchise was on the verge of financial implosion. Without the mega-budget of competing teams across the country, they couldn't afford the big-name players fans loved—the home run hitters, the best-stat pitchers or the game-winning gloves.

Upon examining the numbers, Beane realized that he—and the rest of the world of baseball—had been focusing on the wrong statistics. He discovered that on-base percentage and slugging percentage were better indicators of success on the field. Armed with that knowledge, Beane re-built the team on the franchise's relatively small budget, filling the lineup with players overlooked by other teams because they didn't match the traditional statistical analysis. These players, however, were perfect candidates to produce the statistics Beane was looking for—and cheaper.

William Lamar "Billy" Beane III

Beane's discovery changed everything. Beane's use of sabermetrics—new and improved baseball statistics—took the Oakland Athletics went to the playoffs in 2002 and 2003.

All of the managers knew the numbers. They had knowledge.

Beane knew how to use the numbers to turn the Oakland Athletics into wins. He had wisdom.

Wisdom is the marriage of knowledge and understanding.

When it comes to building character knowledge is good. But wisdom is great.

One of the drawbacks of our educational system is it focuses on ranking students—giving grades, scoring standardized tests, assigning letters and numbers that give us a general understanding of the knowledge a student has obtained. What those tests and report cards don't tell us, however, is a student's passion for learning and understanding.

Knowledge is essential for gaining wisdom. But regurgitating a selection of facts fed to you by others does not demonstrate your ability to think critically, understand, and ask the right questions of yourself and others.

Just like an athlete preparing for a competition, your mind must be exercised if it is to remain fit. It's easy to become lazy and allow other people to do your thinking for you. Strong character comes only from those with strong minds—those who have acquired the knowledge needed, applied wisdom, and come to an understanding of what should be done.

You may not always be in the lead, but when you aren't, you must distinguish yourself as a conscientious follower.

Following other people conscientiously is admirable. Following other people blindly is lazy—and laziness has no place in a life distinguished by excellent character. Think for yourself. Do the hard work of not only acquiring knowledge, but learning.

The best part of knowledge is that which teaches us where our knowledge leaves off, and our ignorance begins.

Here are the facts:

- The first step to knowledge is to realize that you don't know it all.
- What counts in acquiring knowledge is what you learn after you realize and admit that you don't know it all.
- Knowledge knows a fact. Wisdom is knowing what to do with that fact. Knowledge states that a tomato is a fruit. Wisdom knows better than to put it in a fruit salad.
- A good part of knowledge is gained by learning humility and trust.

A lot of people grow up physically, but their growth in knowledge and understanding is stunted—and their success in life reflects that. It's never too late to begin learning again. Learning is a lifelong pursuit that doesn't end with a diploma, or a job, or letters beside your name.

Here are some quick checkpoints for yourself:

- Realize that you do not have all the knowledge you need. Yes, really. The moment you decide you know as much as you need to, your learning adventure will end.
- Refuse to believe that you know it all. There is always something new to learn, something worth learning.
- Learn humility and trust. This will allow you to look past yourself and put your confidence in God. Only then will you add wisdom to your knowledge.

Read through these scriptures

2 Chronicles 1:10 "Give me now wisdom and knowledge, that I may go out and come in before this people: for who can judge this thy people, [that is so] great?"

2 Chronicles 1:11 "And God said to Solomon, Because this was in thine heart, and thou hast not asked riches, wealth, or honour, nor the life of thine enemies, neither yet hast asked long life; but hast asked wisdom and knowledge for thyself, that thou mayest judge my people, over whom I have made thee king:"

2 Chronicles 1:12 "Wisdom and knowledge [is] granted unto thee; and I will give thee riches, and wealth, and honour, such as none of the kings have had that [have been] before thee, neither shall there any after thee have the like."

Psalms 119:66 "Teach me good judgment and knowledge: for I have believed thy commandments.

Proverbs 1:7 "The fear of the LORD [is] the beginning of knowledge: [but] fools despise wisdom and instruction."

Proverbs 2:3 "Yea, if thou criest after knowledge, [and] liftest up thy voice for understanding;"

Proverbs 2:4 "If thou seekest her as silver, and searchest for her as [for] hid treasures;"

Proverbs 2:5 "Then shalt thou understand the fear of the LORD, and find the knowledge of God."

Proverbs 2:6 "For the LORD giveth wisdom: out of his mouth [cometh] knowledge and understanding."

Proverbs 2:10 "When wisdom entereth into thine heart, and knowledge is pleasant unto thy soul;"

Proverbs 2:11 "Discretion shall preserve thee, understanding shall keep thee:"

Proverbs 9:10 "The fear of the LORD [is] the beginning of wisdom: and the knowledge of the holy [is] understanding."

Proverbs 11:9 "An hypocrite with [his] mouth destroyeth his neighbour: but through knowledge shall the just be delivered."

Proverbs 12:1 "Whoso loveth instruction loveth knowledge:"

Proverbs 14:18 "The simple inherit folly: but the prudent are crowned with knowledge."

Proverbs 15:2 "The tongue of the wise useth knowledge aright: but the mouth of fools poureth out foolishness."

Ecclesiastes 2:26 "For [God] giveth to a man that [is] good in his sight wisdom, and knowledge,

Ecclesiastes 7:12 "For wisdom [is] a defence, [and] money [is] a defence: but the excellency of knowledge [is, that] wisdom giveth life to them that have it."

Isaiah 33:6 "And wisdom and knowledge shall be the stability of thy times, [and] strength of salvation: the fear of the LORD [is] his treasure."

Jeremiah 3:15 "And I will give you pastors according to mine heart, which shall feed you with knowledge and understanding."

Daniel 1:17 "As for these four children, God gave them knowledge and skill in all learning and wisdom: and Daniel had understanding in all visions and dreams."

Daniel 2:20 "Daniel answered and said, Blessed be the name of God for ever and ever: for wisdom and might are his:"

Daniel 2:21 "And he changeth the times and the seasons: he removeth kings, and setteth up kings: he giveth wisdom unto the wise, and knowledge to them that know understanding:"

Hosea 4:6 "My people are destroyed for lack of knowledge: because thou hast rejected knowledge, I will also reject thee."

Romans 1:28 "And even as they did not like to retain God in [their] knowledge, God gave them over to a reprobate mind, to do those things which are not convenient;"

Romans 10:2 "For I bear them record that they have a zeal of God, but not according to knowledge."

2 Corinthians 4:6 "For God, who commanded the light to shine out of darkness, hath shined in our hearts, to [give] the light of the knowledge of the glory of God in the face of Jesus Christ."

Ephesians 1:17 "That the God of our Lord Jesus Christ, the Father of glory, may give unto you the spirit of wisdom and revelation in the knowledge of him:"

Ephesians 1:18 "The eyes of your understanding being enlightened; that ye may know what is the hope of his calling, and what the riches of the glory of his inheritance in the saints…"

Colossians 1:9 "For this cause we also, since the day we heard [it], do not cease to pray for you, and to desire that ye might be filled with the knowledge of his will in all wisdom and spiritual understanding;"

Colossians 1:10 "That ye might walk worthy of the Lord unto all pleasing, being fruitful in every good work, and increasing in the knowledge of God;"

Colossians 3:10 "And have put on the new [man], which is renewed in knowledge after the image of him that created him:"

1 Timothy 2:4 "Who will have all men to be saved, and to come unto the knowledge of the truth."

Think through and check the box that fits what you think

1. Ignorance will be no excuse for lack of spiritual understanding and attainment; for we are exhorted to add to virtue, knowledge.

1) ☐ strongly agree   2) ☐ agree   3) ☐ neutral   4) ☐ disagree   5) ☐ strongly disagree

2. Many are very ignorant of Bible truth, and they do not realize the duty and necessity of becoming intelligent Christians.

1) ☐ strongly agree   2) ☐ agree   3) ☐ neutral   4) ☐ disagree   5) ☐ strongly disagree

3. The disciples learned of Jesus, and men perceived the benefits of his association and service, as they saw the change in these men.

1) ☐ strongly agree   2) ☐ agree   3) ☐ neutral   4) ☐ disagree   5) ☐ strongly disagree

4. The uncultured fishermen became men of refinement and ability; and the lessons that they were privileged to learn are written for our admonition and instruction.

1) ☐ strongly agree   2) ☐ agree   3) ☐ neutral   4) ☐ disagree   5) ☐ strongly disagree

5. We are invited to become learners in the school of Christ. We need to acquire all the knowledge possible. We cannot afford to be ignorant of the things that pertain to our eternal welfare.

1) ☐ strongly agree   2) ☐ agree   3) ☐ neutral   4) ☐ disagree   5) ☐ strongly disagree

6. Cease gossip and evil communication, and devote the time to contemplation of Christ and the plan of salvation, they would add the knowledge essential to a growth in grace. We are to add knowledge from "whatsoever things are pure, whatsoever things are lovely, whatsoever things are of good report."

1) ☐ strongly agree   2) ☐ agree   3) ☐ neutral   4) ☐ disagree   5) ☐ strongly disagree

7. God wants us to understand why he has placed us in the world, and given us the sacred burden of life to bear. He would have us develop the faculties of mind and body, that we may be a blessing to those around us, and that his glory may be reflected from us to the world.

1) ☐ strongly agree   2) ☐ agree   3) ☐ neutral   4) ☐ disagree   5) ☐ strongly disagree

8. It is not his will that our powers should be bound up in torpid stupidity and ignorance. "God is light, and in him is no

1) ☐ strongly agree   2) ☐ agree   3) ☐ neutral   4) ☐ disagree   5) ☐ strongly disagree

Highlight thoughts below that expresses what you believe

"The fear of the Lord is the beginning of wisdom, and the knowledge of the holy is understanding"[PROV. 9:10.] The great work of life is Character-building; and a knowledge of God is the foundation of all true education. To impart this knowledge, and to mold the character in harmony with it, should be the object of the teacher's work. The law of God is a reflection of his character. Hence the psalmist says, "All thy commandments are righteousness;"[PS. 119:172.] and "through thy precepts I get understanding."[PS. 119:104.] God has revealed himself to us in his word and in the works of creation. Through the volume of inspiration and the book of nature, we are to obtain a knowledge of God. *CED.065.001*

The knowledge of God as revealed in Christ is the knowledge that all who are saved must have. It is the knowledge that works transformation of character. This knowledge, received, will re-create the soul in the image of God. It will impart to the whole being a spiritual power that is divine. *8T.289.003*

Without health no one can as distinctly understand or as completely fulfill his obligations to himself, to his fellow beings, or to his Creator. Therefore the health should be as faithfully guarded as the CHARACTER. A knowledge of physiology and hygiene should be the basis of all educational effort. *ED.195.002*

The knowledge of God as revealed in Christ is the knowledge that all who are saved must have. It is the knowledge that works transformation of character. This knowledge, received, will re-create the soul in the image of God. It will impart to the whole being a spiritual power that is divine. *MH.425.003*

Without a knowledge of God, humanity would be eternally lost. *PK.693.002* The great work of life is character building, and a knowledge of God is the foundation of all true education. *PP.596.002*

Every temptation resisted, every trial bravely borne, gives us a new experience, and advances us in the work of Character-building. We have a better knowledge of the working of Satan, and of our own power to defeat him through divine grace. *RH.1885-11-24.013*

If you would know how to imitate the spotless life and character of Christ, obtain a knowledge of him as presented in the word of God. *ST.1879-03-06.005*

If you would know how to imitate the spotless life and character of Christ, obtain a knowledge of him as presented in the word of God. *YI.1879-02-19.004*

We must strive to develop a Christian character. Our spiritual understanding must be cleansed, purified, sanctified, and ennobled. All are now taking sides. It is ours now to choose a blessing or a curse. Now is the time for us to purify our minds by obeying the truth. *RH.1899-09-19.011*

Those who are attaining to holiness, are daily growing in love, in meekness, in patience, and in loveliness of character. As faith increases, holiness grows in the soul. As the knowledge of God is enlarged, love is increased, because God is love. *ST.1890-02-24.005*

We should walk humbly with God, make no proud boasts of perfection of character, but in simple faith claim every promise in the word of God; for they are for the obedient, not for the transgressors of God's law. *ST.1890-03-31.007*

CHAPTER 4

SELF-CONTROL

You're sitting in front of your desk at work, staring at your computer screen. There's a project you need to finish for your boss, but it's mid-afternoon, your brain is still at lunch, and no amount of coffee is going to resurrect your creativity. Your procrastination skills, however, have reached Jedi status. You browse YouTube and find videos on how to perfect your pirate accent. You post memes to Facebook, and Tweet about the sound your co-worker makes when she's chewing. You scroll through your favorite entertainment and humor sites, and before you know it, your afternoon's gone, your project is unfinished, and your boss is not happy. So much for self-control.

That's probably what inspired Rawson Marshall Thurber to create a series of funny commercials for Reebok featuring fictional football player "Terrible" Terry Tate as the "office linebacker." In the commercials, the company CEO hires a football linebacker to "inspire" employees lacking self-discipline to stop socializing, make more coffee when the pot is empty, put their aluminum cans in the recycling container instead of the trash, and otherwise conduct themselves properly while at the office.

"Terrible" Terry Tate

Out of nowhere, Terry Tate suddenly tackles unsuspecting employees who are disobeying the rules, wasting time, or taking extra-long breaks. "Since Terry has been with us," the company CEO explains to the camera earnestly, "Our productivity has gone up 46 percent."

Something tells me if it weren't for the Occupational Safety and Health Administration; some real company CEOs would be tempted to try out an office linebacker of their own.

When we talk about self-control, we're not talking about external boundaries. We're not talking about linebackers that keep us on task, or guard the boundaries of our marriages, or help us say "no" to an extra few hundred calories. We're talking about developing a discipline that operates from the inside out.

Self-control—society is full of people who lack that dimension of character. Maybe you know someone who binges on alcohol every weekend, or complains about an expanding waistline while downing another bag of chips. Perhaps you know someone whose credit cards are maxed out because her closets are full of shoes and purses she found on sale. Maybe you know a guy who perfects his pickup lines on every attractive girl he sees, making her feel special for one night only.

Maybe you know someone who is addicted to pornography. Maybe you know someone who can go from nice to nasty—and back—in less time than it took you to read this sentence.

Leaders are in the news all of the time for lewd conduct or embezzled funds, or performance-enhancing drugs. If your goal in life is to pursue pleasure and avoid pain, it's easy to get caught up in destructive shortcuts.

You're probably thinking of someone now who can't control their cravings, their urges, their crushes or their desires. Maybe that someone is you. It's easy to turn on the TV; watch reality shows with bad girls whose claws are always out and who mistake sexual promiscuity for feminist power plays. Or bad boys who party hard and make fools of themselves, and who can't hold down real jobs, and play a comparison game. It's easy to make yourself look disciplined and responsible next to those who appear to many like idiots.

Look at yourself again. Your self-discipline issues might not be as obvious, but you have them. We all do on different levels.

Some people are naturally better equipped to control their impulses than others—but every person's self-discipline has its breaking point. Every person has a limit after which they are a slave to an impulse.

What are you a slave to? Do you have control of your mouth? How about your refrigerator? Your sexual impulses? Money? Your past? Drugs? Alcohol? Bitterness? Jealousy? Anger? What are your triggers that cause you to lose self-control? What are you trying to say "no" to right now? Or later today at dinner, or tonight when that phone call comes?

Strength of character is made up of two things—power of will and power of self-control. Some people mistake strong passion for strength of character, but the truth is that anyone who has been mastered by his or her passions is a very weak person. The real greatness and nobility of a person is measured by that person's powers to subdue strong feelings, not by the controlling power of those feelings in the first place.

Viktor Emil Frankl, a Jewish psychiatrist who spent time in Nazi concentration camps during World War II, has been quoted as saying: "They stripped me naked. They took everything—my wedding ring, watch. I stood there naked and all of a sudden realized at that moment that although they could take everything away from me—my wife, my family, my possessions—they could not take away my freedom to choose how I was going to respond."7

Viktor Emil Frankl

Frankl shows us surrendered self-control at its best. Truly great men and women in this world also possess great self-control. By means of this, all the other dimensions of their character are kept in check and balance.

How do you measure up in terms of self-control? Is it bringing balance to your life and character? As you work through the by-products of self-control, look for anything that might be keeping you from achieving your "best self." Although it is easy to identify extreme examples of the lack of self-control—the violent spouse, the drug-addicted individual, the bankrupt gambler—it isn't wise to say we have no self-control issues. We all do. You do. I do. We are usually blind to our own.

First ask yourself these questions

- What am I trying to say no to right now?
- What am I a slave to?" (Food? Money? Alcohol? Anger? Lust? Power? Laziness? Jealousy? Bitterness? Selfishness?) Give it a name.
- Second, take these steps to establish self-control in your life:
- Track your history with this issue. How successful have you been as you tried to keep it under control? Have you given up trying?
- Surrender those desires. Understand that you don't have the strength on your own, and you need the help of a higher power.
- Give your whole self to the pursuit of self-control. Practice in increments.

Read through these scriptures

Galatians 5:22 "But the fruit of the Spirit is love, joy, peace, longsuffering, gentleness, goodness, faith,
Galatians 5:23 "Meekness, temperance: against such there is no law."

2 Chronicles 30:8 "Now be ye not stiffnecked, as your fathers [were, but] yield yourselves unto the LORD, and enter into his sanctuary, which he hath sanctified for ever: and serve the LORD your God, that the fierceness of his wrath may turn away from you.

Romans 6:12 "Let not sin therefore reign in your mortal body, that ye should obey it in the lusts thereof.

Romans 6:13 "Neither yield ye your members [as] instruments of unrighteousness unto sin: but yield yourselves unto God, as those that are alive from the dead, and your members [as] instruments of righteousness unto God.

Romans 6:14 "For sin shall not have dominion over you: for ye are not under the law, but under grace."

Romans 6:15 "What then? shall we sin, because we are not under the law, but under grace? God forbid."

Romans 6:16 "Know ye not, that to whom ye yield yourselves servants to obey, his servants ye are to whom ye obey; whether of sin unto death, or of obedience unto righteousness?

Romans 6:17 But God be thanked, that ye were the servants of sin, but ye have obeyed from the heart that form of doctrine which was delivered you.

Romans 6:19 I speak after the manner of men because of the infirmity of your flesh: for as ye have yielded your members servants to uncleanness and to iniquity unto iniquity; even so now yield your members servants to righteousness unto holiness.

Romans 6:20 For when ye were the servants of sin, ye were free from righteousness.

Romans 6:21 What fruit had ye then in those things whereof ye are now ashamed? for the end of those things [is] death.

Romans 6:22 But now being made free from sin, and become servants to God, ye have your fruit unto holiness, and the end everlasting life.

John 8:31 Then said Jesus to those Jews which believed on him, If ye continue in my word, [then] are ye my disciples indeed;

John 8:32 And ye shall know the truth, and the truth shall make you free.

John 8:33 They answered him, We be Abraham's seed, and were never in bondage to any man: how sayest thou, Ye shall be made free?

John 8:34 Jesus answered them, Verily, verily, I say unto you, Whosoever committeth sin is the servant of sin.

1. Strength of character consists of two things--power of will and power of self-control.

1) ☐ strongly agree   2) ☐ agree   3) ☐ neutral   4) ☐ disagree   5) ☐ strongly disagree

2. The real greatness of the man is measured by the power of the feelings that he controls, not by those that control him.

1) ☐ strongly agree   2) ☐ agree   3) ☐ neutral   4) ☐ disagree   5) ☐ strongly disagree

3. It is next to an impossibility for an intemperate person to be patient.

1) ☐ strongly agree   2) ☐ agree   3) ☐ neutral   4) ☐ disagree   5) ☐ strongly disagree

4. Appetite, passion, and love of display are carrying multitudes into the greatest excesses and extravagance.

1) ☐ strongly agree   2) ☐ agree   3) ☐ neutral   4) ☐ disagree   5) ☐ strongly disagree

5. Youth is the time to acquire knowledge for daily practice through life; a right character may then be easily formed. It is the time to establish good habits, to gain and to hold the power of self-control. Youth is the sowing time, and the seed sown determines the harvest, both for this life and the life to come.

1) ☐ strongly agree   2) ☐ agree   3) ☐ neutral   4) ☐ disagree   5) ☐ strongly disagree

6. The highest evidence of nobility in a Christian is self-control. He who under abuse or cruelty fails to maintain a calm and trustful spirit robs God of His right to reveal in him His own perfection of character.

1) ☐ strongly agree   2) ☐ agree   3) ☐ neutral   4) ☐ disagree   5) ☐ strongly disagree

7. Self-control is essential to living a life of holiness

1) ☐ strongly agree   2) ☐ agree   3) ☐ neutral   4) ☐ disagree   5) ☐ strongly disagree

Highlight thoughts below that expresses what you believe

Build upon Jesus Christ; He is the one sure foundation. "Other foundation can no man lay than that is laid, which is Jesus Christ." His strength of character is sufficient for you. In Christ, the Word of God gives you the right of way to spiritual blessing; but it is a way of self-denial and self-sacrifice; it is a way of self-control and self-discipline. The character of Christ may become your character; His spirit, your spirit. *AU.1907-04-29.005*

Many mistake strong passions for a strong character but the truth is that he who is mastered by his passions is a weak man. *PP.568.001*

The life of Daniel is an inspired illustration of what constitutes a sanctified character. It presents a lesson for all, and especially for the young. A strict compliance with the requirements of God is beneficial to the health of body and mind. In order to reach the highest standard of moral and intellectual attainments, it is necessary to seek wisdom and strength from God and to observe strict temperance in all the habits of life. *SL.023.002*

Self-control is absolutely essential to the proper education of our children. The want of this quality of character is the key to the horrible records of crime chronicled every day by the press. *HR.1878-11-01.005*

It may cost a severe conflict to overcome habits which have been long indulged, but we may triumph through the grace of Christ. He invites us to learn of him. He would have us practice self-control, and be perfect in character working that which is well pleasing in his sight. "By their fruits ye shall know them," is his own standard of judging character. *RH.1884-06-10.011*

In childhood and youth the character is most impressible. The power of self-control should then be acquired. By the fireside and at the family board influences are exerted the results of which are as enduring as eternity. More than any natural endowment, the habits established in early years will decide whether a man shall be victorious or vanquished in the battle of life. *RH.1907-10-31.006*

Would Jesus require this self-control, if it were not for your real happiness to practice it? No; he wishes you to cultivate such traits of character as will bring peace to your own hearts, and enable you to brighten other hearts and lives with the sunshine of love, joy, and cheerful contentment. *YI.1884-01-30.002*

God's abounding love and presence in the heart will give the power of self-control, and will mold and fashion the mind and character. *YI.1907-11-12.008*

A child's first school should be his home. His first instructors should be his father and his mother. His first lessons should be the lessons of respect, obedience, reverence and self-control. If he is not instructed aright by his parent, Satan will instruct him in evil through agencies that are most objectionable. How important, then, is the school in the home! Here the character is first shaped. Here the destiny of souls is often largely influenced. Even the parents who are endeavoring to do their best, have not a hundredth part of the realization they should have of the value of a human soul. *SPM.264.001*

Day by day the character grows into the likeness of Christ, and finally, instead of being the sport of circumstances, instead of indulging selfishness, and being carried away by light and trifling conversation, the man is master of his thoughts and words. It may cost a severe conflict to overcome habits which have been long indulged, but we may triumph through the grace of Christ. He invites us to learn of him. He would have us practice self-control, and be perfect in character working that which is well-pleasing in his sight. "By their fruits ye shall know them,"[MATT. 7:20.] is his own standard of judging character. *GW92.421.001*

The imagination must be positively and persistently controlled if the passions and affections are made subject to reason, conscience, and character. *2T.562.002*

Many have received, as their birthright, both strong and weak points of character which are positive defects. These peculiarities color the entire life. *4T.361.001*

CHAPTER 5

PATIENCE

He was born in prison. When his mother was five months pregnant with him, she was arrested in connection with a murder in India—a charge she denied. Although she was sentenced to life in prison, she appealed her case and was granted bail while she waited for her appeal. But no one came to post bail for her—not her husband, or any other member of her family—so she waited in prison. For 19 years. At the age of six, Kanhaiya was taken from his mother and sent to a remand home. He was scared and lonely. "I was very sad," he told reporters. "Without her, I had no one my me.

Kanhaiya never forgot about his mother. Seven years later, when he was finally released from the remand home, he immediately went to work at a garment factory. He worked hard, day shifts and night shifts, in order to raise the 5,000 rupees ($89) necessary to help his mother get out of prison on bail. It took six years.

Nineteen years after his mother was arrested, Kanhaiya brought the money he had saved and freed his mother from prison.

Patience. It's the dimension of character that gives birth to perseverance. In classical Greek, the word for perseverance is hypomone [Strong's Concordance] and it describes the ability of a plant to thrive in a harsh environment—literally in the deserts and on rocky slopes. Like that little clump of grass in the harsh environment of a muddy Lake, Kanhaiya had hypomon, perseverance. He did not give up trying to rescue his mother.

Men and women of strong character do not quit when difficulties occur. To be patient means you don't give up. When you are provoked, you don't quit. You forbear and you persevere. In later Greek and Jewish literature, hypomone was used to refer to the spiritual staying power of a person's character. If people do not have patience, forbearance, and perseverance, they cannot reach their God-given destiny.

Anyone who has ever tried to do anything difficult, anything of value that requires intestinal fortitude, has been tempted to throw in the towel. People of strong character will sometimes become discouraged, but they will never give up. They have learned from previous experience that anything worth having requires some effort and endurance to obtain.

Patience and perseverance build character, and character makes the person. You are your character. The people who succeed are the ones who have developed the kind of character that won't quit.

People with a victim mentality use difficult circumstances to give up. Successful people recognize difficult circumstances as opportunities to toughen up, to learn, to grow, and get stronger. It is in the quiet crucible of our personal, private sufferings that our noblest dreams are born, and

God's greatest gifts are given—often given in compensation for what we've been through.

Life requires perseverance and endurance, not short bursts of good intentions. So learn to push aside those things that weigh you down, divert your attention, sap your energy, or dampen your enthusiasm. Say to yourself, "I will not give up. I will not give in. I will not give out."

The person who patiently endures succeeds.

A couple of years before his successful attempt to be the first to scale Mount Everest, the fa-mous explorer from New Zealand, Sir Edmund Hillary, failed in an earlier, British-sponsored effort. Neverthe-less, he and his team returned to London to a hero's wel-come, and a banquet was held in their honor. Behind the speaker's platform, they had hung a huge blown-up photograph of Mount Everest.

Sir Edmund Hillary

When Hillary rose to receive the acclaim of the distin-guished audience, he turned around, faced, the picture, and said, "Mount Everest, you have defeated me. But I will return! And I will defeat you! Because you can't get any bigger ... and I can!" As the world now knows, he did.

Patience and perseverance means that you keep be-lieving, but they also mean you continue working while you keep the hope alive. Too often, we give up quickly. When the days stretch out into years, and you're tired, and you want to give up, a person with patience will say; "No matter how long it takes, no matter how difficult or painful it becomes, no matter how many discourage-ments and disappointments and obstacles I have to face, I'm not going to give up. Ever. If I don't give up, I will see success come out of failure and victory come out of defeat. If I give up too soon, I may miss my blessing. I'm not going to give up on my education, my dream, my career, my mar-riage, my health, my finances...."

If you persevere with patience, you will take into your future not only triumph after triumph, but also a stronger, more robust character.

On February 19, 1979, Norman Ollestad's father chartered a small plane to take them over the San Gabriel Mountains to Big Bear, where Norm, who was a young ski champion, was to receive an award. With the eleven-year-old boy, his dad, and the pilot was his father's girlfriend, Sandra.

Norm recalls the events of that day: A few minutes into the flight ... we hit the storm. All the win-dows were gray. You couldn't see up or down, left or right. Pretty soon, a limb flashed by the win-dow, and I thought, "Well, it's a trick of light, something. It's funny, because limbs aren't up in the sky...." Then I knew we were about to crash. I curled up my body and yelled, "Watch out," and there were a couple of thuds. Went right through my spine. Then the next thing I knew I woke up and the plane was torn apart."[8]

They were hanging over the edge of an ice chute. Norm tried to rouse his dad, but found that he was dead, along with the pilot. Sandra was alive, but badly injured, and as the two of them tried to get away from the teetering wreck, she plunged into the chute to her death.

Young Norm was on his own. For nine hours, Norm slipped and climbed down the storm-locked mountain. He reached some level ground, where he found footprints in the snow, and he followed them to a road, where he was rescued.

Many years later, after Norm had become a father himself, he wrote a book about the accident, Crazy for the Storm: A Memoir of Survival. In it, he credits his father with instilling in him the never-give-up grit that he needed on that dreadful day. Without his father's persistent coaching in perseverance, Norm knows he would never have attempted to climb off that mountain by himself.

The author Annie Dillard once wrote, "You don't have to sit outside in the dark. If, however, you want to look at the stars, darkness is necessary."9 Darkness is a given, a normal part of the human experience. But the stars will be shining anyway, whether you notice them or not. If you embrace the darkness, you will see and experience things sitting in the dark that you never did in the light.

In each of our lives, there is a limp, some inadequacy or disfigurement. Nobody gets it all perfect. Perhaps in your life you have never found enough love or compassion. Or perhaps you've always been passed over and misunderstood. All around the world, people are being overwhelmed by some insufficiency. People are strained to their limits economically and emotionally, and they feel trapped by their weakness, mired in a sense of failure.

We can't seem to get enough of whatever it takes to make us truly happy and secure. That's why, today more than ever, patience and perseverance are needed.

Always remember that character is the result of the hard work of construction. Character cannot be bought, sold, or traded. It must be forged on the anvil of sweat and effort. Tragedy and trouble must not be a foreign language. Time will prove the worth of the trials and new life will replace the old.

People of strong character are not quitters. In the face of difficulties, they press forward patiently. They persevere. They overcome. The two words, patience, and perseverance are closely related. Perseverance may "sweat" a little more, but it means patient hard work.

Patience will help you handle what is happening now, while perseverance will help you handle situations that are protracted.

Patience will hold you together while perseverance keeps you going. If you persevere with patience, you will experience not only triumph after triumph, but you will also be rewarded with a stronger, more robust character.

Here are some of the steps you can take to increase your patience and perseverance. They are drawn from the lives of those who have proven their strength in this important element of divine character:

• Exercise your will to get back on your feet when you fall down. Your mistakes can't stop you if you don't let them.

• Learn from your failures and keep going.

• Refuse to waste time wishing for a rosy, easy life. Instead, appreciate the fact that your trials and difficulties make you stronger inside.

• Remember that rewards lie ahead. You can outlast your troubles, no matter how complicated they seem to be.

Read through these scriptures

Luke 8:15 "But that on the good ground are they, which in an honest and good heart, having heard the word, keep [it], and bring forth fruit with patience."

Luke 21:19 "In your patience possess ye your souls."

Romans 5:3 "And not only [so], but we glory in tribulations also: knowing that tribulation worketh patience;"

Romans 5:4 "And patience, experience; and experience, hope:"

Romans 8:25 "But if we hope for that we see not, [then] do we with patience wait for [it]."

Romans 15:4 "For whatsoever things were written aforetime were written for our learning, that we through patience and comfort of the scriptures might have hope.

Romans 15:5 "Now the God of patience and consolation grant you to be likeminded one toward another according to Christ Jesus:

2 Corinthians 6:4 "But in all [things] approving ourselves as the ministers of God, in much patience, in afflictions, in necessities, in distresses,

2 Corinthians 12:12 "Truly the signs of an apostle were wrought among you in all patience, in signs, and wonders, and mighty deeds."

Colossians 1:11 "Strengthened with all might, according to his glorious power, unto all patience and longsuffering with joyfulness;"

1 Thessalonians 1:3 "Remembering without ceasing your work of faith, and labour of love, and patience of hope in our Lord Jesus Christ, in the sight of God and our Father;"

2. Thessalonians 1:4 "So that we ourselves glory in you in the churches of God for your patience and faith in all your persecutions and tribulations that ye endure:"

1 Timothy 6:11 "But thou, O man of God, flee these things; and follow after righteousness, godliness, faith, love, patience, meekness."

2 Timothy 3:10 "But thou hast fully known my doctrine, manner of life, purpose, faith, longsuffering, charity, patience,"

Titus 2:2 "That the aged men be sober, grave, temperate, sound in faith, in charity, in patience."

Hebrews 6:12 "That ye be not slothful, but followers of them who through faith and patience inherit the promises."

Hebrews 10:36 "For ye have need of patience, that, after ye have done the will of God, ye might receive the promise."

Hebrews 12:1 "Wherefore seeing we also are compassed about with so great a cloud of witnesses, let us lay aside every weight, and the sin which doth so easily beset [us], and let us run with patience the race that is set before us,"

James 1:3 "Knowing [this], that the trying of your faith worketh patience."

James 1:4 "But let patience have [her] perfect work, that ye may be perfect and entire, wanting nothing."

James 5:7 "Be patient therefore, brethren, unto the coming of the Lord. Behold, the husbandman waiteth for the precious fruit of the earth, and hath long patience for it, until he receive the early and latter rain."

James 5:10 "Take, my brethren, the prophets, who have spoken in the name of the Lord, for an example of suffering affliction, and of patience."

James 5:11 "Behold, we count them happy which endure. Ye have heard of the patience of Job, and have seen the end of the Lord; that the Lord is very pitiful, and of tender mercy."

2. Peter 1:6 " And to knowledge temperance; and to temperance patience; and to patience god-liness;"

Revelation 1:9 "I John, who also am your brother, and companion in tribulation, and in the kingdom and patience of Jesus Christ, was in the isle that is called Patmos, for the word of God, and for the testimony of Jesus Christ."

Revelation 2:2 "I know thy works, and thy labour, and thy patience, and how thou canst not bear them which are evil: and thou hast tried them which say they are apostles, and are not, and hast found them liars:"

Revelation 2:3 "And hast borne, and hast patience, and for my name's sake hast laboured, and hast not fainted."

Revelation 2:19 "I know thy works, and charity, and service, and faith, and thy patience, and thy works; and the last [to be] more than the first."

Revelation 3:10 "Because thou hast kept the word of my patience, I also will keep thee from the hour of temptation, which shall come upon all the world, to try them that dwell upon the earth."

Revelation 13:10 "He that leadeth into captivity shall go into captivity: he that killeth with the sword must be killed with the sword. Here is the patience and the faith of the saints."

Revelation 14:12 "Here is the patience of the saints: here [are] they that keep the commandments of God, and the faith of Jesus."

Think through and check the box that fits what you think

1. Impatience brings strife and accusation and sorrow; but patience pours the balm of peace and love into the experiences of the home life.
1) ☐ strongly agree   2) ☐ agree   3) ☐ neutral   4) ☐ disagree   5) ☐ strongly disagree

2. When we exercise the precious grace of patience toward others, they will reflect our spirit, and we shall gather with Christ.
1) ☐ strongly agree   2) ☐ agree   3) ☐ neutral   4) ☐ disagree   5) ☐ strongly disagree

3. Patience will seek for unity in the church, in the family, and in the community. This grace must be woven into our lives. Everyone should mount this round of progress, and add to faith, virtue, and temperance, the grace of patience.
1) ☐ strongly agree   2) ☐ agree   3) ☐ neutral   4) ☐ disagree   5) ☐ strongly disagree

4. You can represent the character of Christ by your patience...
1) ☐ strongly agree   2) ☐ agree   3) ☐ neutral   4) ☐ disagree   5) ☐ strongly disagree

5. We should possess the attributes of Christ's character one of which is patience...
1) ☐ strongly agree   2) ☐ agree   3) ☐ neutral   4) ☐ disagree   5) ☐ strongly disagree

6. The wisdom of God brings patience.
1) ☐ strongly agree   2) ☐ agree   3) ☐ neutral   4) ☐ disagree   5) ☐ strongly disagree

7. Patience is one of the evidences of the Character of Christ.
1) ☐ strongly agree   2) ☐ agree   3) ☐ neutral   4) ☐ disagree   5) ☐ strongly disagree

8. We should weave patience into the fabric of our CHARACTER the threads of patience.
1) ☐ strongly agree   2) ☐ agree   3) ☐ neutral   4) ☐ disagree   5) ☐ strongly disagree

9. The opposition we meet develops patience

1) ☐ strongly agree   2) ☐ agree   3) ☐ neutral   4) ☐ disagree   5) ☐ strongly disagree

Highlight thoughts below that expresses what you believe

"Without Me," says Christ, "ye can do nothing;" but with His divine grace working through our human efforts, we can do all things. His patience and meekness will pervade the character, diffusing a precious radiance which makes bright and clear the pathway to heaven. By beholding and imitating His life we shall become renewed in His image. The glory of heaven will shine in our lives and be reflected upon others. At the throne of grace we are to find the help we need to enable us to live thus. This is genuine sanctification, and what more exalted position can mortals desire than to be connected with Christ as a branch is joined to the vine? *5T.307.001*

The Christian youth should be in earnest, trained to bear responsibilities with brave heart and willing hand. He should be ready to encounter the trials of life with patience and fortitude. He should seek to form a character after the model of the divine One, following maxims of worth, confirming himself in habits that will enable him to win the victor's crown. *CED.089.001*

The study of the Bible will ennoble every thought, feeling, and aspiration as no other study can. It gives stability of purpose, patience, courage, and fortitude; it refines the character and sanctifies the soul. *GC.094.003*

The character of Christ is full of forbearance, patience, goodness, mercy, and unexampled love. By beholding such a character, they will rise above the littleness of that which has fashioned and molded them, and made them unholy and unlovely. *RH.1894-01-16.008*

We are to be faithful soldiers, obeying the orders of the Captain of our salvation. We are not to take the Captain's place; but hourly to live in constant contact with Christ. We must know, individually, that we know the truth, not only theoretically, but practically. We must bring its divine principles into our daily life. God requires truth in the inward parts, and in the hidden part wisdom. He requires us to practise righteousness, to manifest patience, mercy, and love. We should carefully review our character in the light of the character of God, as expressed in his holy law. There should be no deviating from the perfect standard. The Lord says, "Be ye therefore perfect, even as your Father which is in heaven is perfect." *RH.1897-11-30.00*9

It takes time and patience to grow in Christlikeness of character; but it is a very easy matter to accept the attributes of Satan, and fall into his ways. *RH.1899-01-03.017*

Every Christian must be a learner in the school of Christ; and there is need of diligent and persevering effort to reach that standard of righteousness which God's word requires. Every one has a work to do to learn the lessons of justice, humility, patience, purity, and love. These traits of character are more precious in the sight of our Lord than offerings of gold or silver. They are more acceptable to him than the most costly sacrifice. *LP.233.001*

CHAPTER 6

REVERENCE AND SACREDNESS

What is sacred to you?

Your marriage? Your time with your kids? Your religious or political beliefs? Your personal space? Ridding the world of injustice? Being a voice for the voiceless? Life?

We have come to a time when the idea of sacredness or something being holy, has been virtually expunged from our common vocabulary. Not only has it been drained from our lives, but it has been replaced by a sense of irreverence. We turn on TV and watch comedians make fun of everything. Society has made us feel ashamed of holding anything as holy—as though valuing anything as sacred indicates a form of weakness. Sometimes we laugh, and it sounds hollow to our own ears, and something inside us says, "They shouldn't make fun of that. It's sacred."

All of us have an internal sense of sacredness.

On July 20, 2012, moviegoers filled a theater in Aurora, Colorado to watch a midnight showing of the third installment of the Batman Trilogy, The Dark Knight Rises. They only watched the first 30 minutes of the film. A masked gunman entered the theater in full tactical gear, threw tear gas grenades, and then sprayed the audience with bullets from multiple firearms. Police arrived within 90 seconds, but by then, the theater was already a bloodbath.

Aurora, Colorado

Twelve people were killed—a six year old girl, a father of two, an 18-year-old high school student, an active duty staff sergeant, a world traveler and father, an aspiring sports journalist, a naval petty officer, a community college student, a 27-year-old man who died protecting his girlfriend, a man celebrating his 27th birthday, a recent University of Denver graduate, and an Air Force member and mother of two—and 58 were injured.

The town, and the entire country, was in shock. A few days later, grieving family members of those killed in the Aurora shootings planned funerals and tried to cope with the horror and loss.

At the same time, a few states away, comedian Dane Cook was performing at the Laugh Factory in Los Angeles.

"I heard that the guy came into the theater about 25 minutes in," Cook reportedly joked to his audience. "And I don't know if you've seen the movie, but the movie's pretty much a piece of crap. Yeah, spoiler alert. I know that if none of that would have happened, I'm pretty sure that somebody in the theater, about 25 minutes in realizing it was a piece of crap, probably was like, 'Ugh, ...shoot me.'"

Cook's words touched a raw nerve for people not only in Aurora, but also across the country. In addition to the news and radio outlets verbally thrashing his audacity, social media outlets created a firestorm, and even hardcore Dane Cook fans condemned his joke. His joke was insensitive. It was untimely. And, for people who had seen the images and felt the pain of the tragedy, it messed with something sacred.

The word profane comes from a Greek word bebeylos, which means, "something coming from what is base." Profaning something sacred is the equivalent of dunking it in sewage. Or joking about it in the Laugh Factory.

An important part of character is the discovery, the appreciation, and the fierce protection of the sacred things in our lives. In forsaking sacredness, we also forsake what it means to be human.

Abraham Herschel, an American rabbi and Jewish theologian said: "The awe we sense or ought to sense when standing in the presence of a human being is a moment of intuition for the likeness of God which is concealed in his essence. Something sacred is at stake in every moment."

Your attitude toward sacred things will constantly be reflected in your words and actions—and people will notice. They will also notice if you have a careless attitude toward things that are sacred. It's a personal choice—but it will affect your relationships, opportunities, accomplishments and every other aspect of your life.

These action steps should help you establish a right inner attitude toward the sacred:
  • Read the Book of Proverbs in the Bible. It was written several thousand years ago, and yet its advice and warnings are amazingly modern when it comes to developing respect and honor.
  • Identify those areas where your attitude needs to change.
  • Ask others to forgive you for your lack of honor and respect when you have not given honor where honor is due.
  • Manage your mouth. Your tongue is the most unruly part of your body, a part that you and only you can control.

Read through these scriptures
  1 Timothy 2:2 "For kings, and [for] all that are in authority; that we may lead a quiet and peaceable life in all godliness and honesty."
  1 Timothy 2:10 "But (which becometh women professing godliness) with good works."
  1 Timothy 3:16 "And without controversy great is the mystery of godliness: God was manifest in the flesh, justified in the Spirit, seen of angels, preached unto the Gentiles, believed on in the world, received up into glory."

1 Timothy 4:7 "But refuse profane and old wives' fables, and exercise thyself [rather] unto godliness."

1 Timothy 4:8 "For bodily exercise profiteth little: but godliness is profitable unto all things, having promise of the life that now is, and of that which is to come."

1 Timothy 6:3 "If any man teach otherwise, and consent not to wholesome words, [even] the words of our Lord Jesus Christ, and to the doctrine which is according to godliness;"

1 Timothy 6:5 "Perverse disputings of men of corrupt minds, and destitute of the truth, supposing that gain is godliness: from such withdraw thyself."

1 Timothy 6:6 "But godliness with contentment is great gain."

1 Timothy 6:11 "But thou, O man of God, flee these things; and follow after righteousness, godliness, faith, love, patience, meekness."

2 Timothy 3:5 "Having a form of godliness, but denying the power thereof: from such turn away."

Titus 1:1 "Paul, a servant of God, and an apostle of Jesus Christ, according to the faith of God's elect, and the acknowledging of the truth which is after godliness;"

2 Peter 1:3 "According as his divine power hath given unto us all things that [pertain] unto life and godliness, through the knowledge of him that hath called us to glory and virtue:"

2 Peter 1:6 "And to knowledge temperance; and to temperance patience; and to patience godliness;

2 Peter 1:7 "And to godliness brotherly kindness; and to brotherly kindness charity."

2 Peter 3:11 "[Seeing] then [that] all these things shall be dissolved, what manner [of persons] ought ye to be in [all] holy conversation and godliness…"

Think through and check the box that fits what you think

1. Godliness is the fruit of Christian character.
1) ☐ strongly agree   2) ☐ agree   3) ☐ neutral   4) ☐ disagree   5) ☐ strongly disagree

3. The wisdom spoken of by the psalmist is that which is attained when the truth is opened to the mind and applied to the heart by the Spirit of God; when its principles are wrought into the character by a life of practical godliness.
1) ☐ strongly agree   2) ☐ agree   3) ☐ neutral   4) ☐ disagree   5) ☐ strongly disagree

4. A character that combines strength and godliness is an unconquerable power for good.
1) ☐ strongly agree   2) ☐ agree   3) ☐ neutral   4) ☐ disagree   5) ☐ strongly disagree

5. God has opened to men the perfection and holiness of His character
1) ☐ strongly agree   2) ☐ agree   3) ☐ neutral   4) ☐ disagree   5) ☐ strongly disagree

6. We represent Christ in true goodness of character
1) ☐ strongly agree   2) ☐ agree   3) ☐ neutral   4) ☐ disagree   5) ☐ strongly disagree

7 We should beautify the truth by holiness of character,
To live the law of God, means to reveal the holiness of God's character in every action of the law.
1) ☐ strongly agree   2) ☐ agree   3) ☐ neutral   4) ☐ disagree   5) ☐ strongly disagree

8. Through repentance and faith we might become like him in holiness of character.
1) ☐ strongly agree   2) ☐ agree   3) ☐ neutral   4) ☐ disagree   5) ☐ strongly disagree

9. We should ever be progressing in holiness and perfection of Christian character.
1) ☐ strongly agree   2) ☐ agree   3) ☐ neutral   4) ☐ disagree   5) ☐ strongly disagree

10. Now is the time to seek purity and holiness of character.

1) ☐ strongly agree   2) ☐ agree   3) ☐ neutral   4) ☐ disagree   5) ☐ strongly disagree

11. Holiness of life and character is a rare thing,

1) ☐ strongly agree   2) ☐ agree   3) ☐ neutral   4) ☐ disagree   5) ☐ strongly disagree

12. Those who exercise true faith in Christ make it manifest by holiness of character,

1) ☐ strongly agree   2) ☐ agree   3) ☐ neutral   4) ☐ disagree   5) ☐ strongly disagree

13. The holiness of his character is reflected by all who serve him in spirit and in truth.

1) ☐ strongly agree   2) ☐ agree   3) ☐ neutral   4) ☐ disagree   5) ☐ strongly disagree

14. Holy, holy, holy, Lord God Almighty. He is declared to be glorious in his holiness.

1) ☐ strongly agree   2) ☐ agree   3) ☐ neutral   4) ☐ disagree   5) ☐ strongly disagree

15. In the kingdom of God nobility and holiness of character are accounted wealth.

1) ☐ strongly agree   2) ☐ agree   3) ☐ neutral   4) ☐ disagree   5) ☐ strongly disagree

16. Jesus was what every Christian should strive to be in holiness and winsomeness of character. Let us learn from him how to combine firmness, purity, and integrity with unselfishness, courtesy, and kindly sympathy.

1) ☐ strongly agree   2) ☐ agree   3) ☐ neutral   4) ☐ disagree   5) ☐ strongly disagree

17. Through the merits and virtues of Jesus Christ, the soul may wear the image of Him who created man in His own likeness. It is holiness of life and Christlikeness of character that constitute the beauty of the soul.

1) ☐ strongly agree   2) ☐ agree   3) ☐ neutral   4) ☐ disagree   5) ☐ strongly disagree

18. The followers of Jesus are to be distinguished by their holiness of character.

1) ☐ strongly agree   2) ☐ agree   3) ☐ neutral   4) ☐ disagree   5) ☐ strongly disagree

29. No man inherits holiness of character by nature,

1) ☐ strongly agree   2) ☐ agree   3) ☐ neutral   4) ☐ disagree   5) ☐ strongly disagree

30. Reverence is an expression of Divine Character.

1) ☐ strongly agree   2) ☐ agree   3) ☐ neutral   4) ☐ disagree   5) ☐ strongly disagree

31. The cultivation of reverence for him will affect the daily life. The entire character will be elevated and transformed.

1) ☐ strongly agree   2) ☐ agree   3) ☐ neutral   4) ☐ disagree   5) ☐ strongly disagree

32. The only safe-guard against these dangers is to add to patience godliness,--to reverence God, his character and his law, and to keep his fear ever before the mind. By communion with God, through prayer and the reading of his word, we should cultivate such a sense of the holiness of his character that we shall regard sin as he regards it.

1) ☐ strongly agree   2) ☐ agree   3) ☐ neutral   4) ☐ disagree   5) ☐ strongly disagree

33. Goodness is character made visible

1) ☐ strongly agree   2) ☐ agree   3) ☐ neutral   4) ☐ disagree   5) ☐ strongly disagree

Highlight thoughts below that expresses what you believe

Holiness is the result of surrendering all to God; it is doing the will of our heavenly Father. *MB.149.002*

When a man has ...."serious defects in his character. He does not have reverence for sacred and holy things; his heart has not been changed by the Spirit of God. He is selfish, boastful, and loves pleasure more than duty. He has no experience in self-denial and humiliation. *3T.042.002*

"Holy and reverend is His name." Psalm 111:9. All should meditate upon His majesty, His purity and holiness, that the heart may be impressed with a sense of His exalted character; and His holy name should be uttered with reverence and solemnity. *PP.307.001*

The Lord our God is holy, and his name is to be treated with great reverence. Angels are displeased and disgusted with the irreverent manner in which the name of God, the great Jehovah, is sometimes used in prayer. They mention that name with the greatest awe, even veiling their faces when they speak the name of God; the name of Christ also is sacred, and is spoken with the greatest reverence. And those who in their prayers use the name of God in a common and flippant manner, have no sense of the exalted character of God, of Christ, or of heavenly things. *ST.1886-11-18.013*

As we learn learn "more of the divine character through the works of creation," ..."reverence for God is increased." *SL.076.001*

All the truths of revelation are of value to us; and in contemplating things of eternal interest, we shall gain true perceptions of the character of God. The cultivation of reverence for him will affect the daily life. The entire character will be elevated and transformed. The soul will be brought into harmony with Heaven. The believer will become Christ-like, and will finally obtain an abundant entrance into the city of God. *ST.1886-06-03.014*

The work of Christ is sacred, and the command is, "Be ye clean, that bear the vessels of the Lord." He requires perfection of character in his agents. *RH.1891-01-27.010*

Truth is sacred, divine. It is stronger and more powerful than anything else in the formation of a character after the likeness of Christ. In it there is fulness of joy. When it is cherished in the heart, the love of Christ is preferred to the love of any human being. This is Christianity. This is the love of God in the soul. Thus pure, unadulterated truth occupies the citadel of the being. The words are fulfilled, "A new heart also will I give you, and a new spirit will I put within you." There is a nobleness in the life of the one who lives and works under the vivifying influence of the truth. *RH.1899-02-14.004*

The character of holiness to which we must attain, Christ has revealed. *AU.1906-10-01.002*

The holiness of his character is reflected by all who serve him in spirit and in truth. *RH.1896-12-22.008*

Moses prayed to God, saying, "I beseech thee, show me thy glory." And God said, "I will make all my goodness pass before thee. . . . And the Lord passed by before him, and proclaimed, The Lord, The Lord God, merciful and gracious, long-suffering, and abundant in goodness and truth, keeping mercy for thousands, forgiving iniquity and transgression and sin, and that will by no means clear the guilty; visiting the iniquity of the fathers upon the children, and upon the children's children, unto the third and to the fourth generation."

In this representation, the Lord desired to teach the lesson that he requires in his people purity of character and holiness of life. *RH.1910-11-10.016*

Those who are attaining to holiness, are daily growing in love, in meekness, in patience, and in loveliness of character. As faith increases, holiness grows in the soul. *ST.1890-02-24.005*

CHAPTER 7

KINDNESS

When the Boston Marathon bombings rocked the nation in April 2013, the images that emerged from the scene of bloody chaos were powerful. And yet, even more powerful than the evil that took place, stories of powerful kindness also began to rise out of the dust and despair to lift our spirits.

Carlos Arrendondo made the national news twice.

The first time was when he found out his son had been killed in Iraq. Shocked by grief, Carlos was devastated and reckless. He got into his van with a gas can and a propane torch, and began splashing gasoline everywhere while the Marines who delivered the news of his son's death helplessly tried to talk him out of his frenzy. The van exploded in flames. Carlos was pulled from the van, but spent the next part of his life strapped to a hospital bed to save him from himself, unconscious at first, but then painfully awake to experience the agony of burn recovery—the bandages, and the feeling of his dead skin being pulled off. After he had recovered from his burns, he lost another son to suicide.

Boston Marathon Bombing

The second time Carlos made the news was after the Boston Marathon bombings. In the desperate seconds following the attack, Carlos acted on instinct. Tearing up pieces of a sweater he'd found on the ground, he began to use them as tourniquets on the bloody stumps of amputees—even retying them when they fell off. He did his best to minimize the horror by reassuring victims they would be all right, and hiding the worst of their injuries from them while he got them help.

Though carrying his own burden of pain, Carlos forgot about himself during his acts of kindness. And in the process, he saved lives. Such is the power of kindness.

Dr. David Hamilton, in his book Why Kindness is Good for You, cites multiple studies supporting claims that kindness has the power to boost your immune system, lift depression, and help your body regenerate faster. Kindness, he says, is a more useful in attracting someone of the opposite sex than physical features.

The seventh secret to a better life is kindness. There's something about us, as human beings, that responds to an act of kindness like nothing else.

After all, we are only flesh and blood, aren't we? We're not steel and iron. We are, for the most part, soft tissue. We are fragile. So fragile, in fact, that sometimes something as simple as a kind word, a kind act, a kind gesture, can make all the difference.

A man told a story about how, not long after he had graduated college; a man approached him in a restaurant. He had known the man from high school well enough to remember his face, if not his name. The man walked up and extended his hand.

"Hi, Jack," he said. "Remember me, Joey Smith from the tenth grade?"

"Yeah," Jack said. "Now I do. How are you?"

"I'm doing OK," Joey said. "And that has a lot to do with you."

"With me? What do you mean?"

"Yes," Joey said. "In fact, I can honestly say that if it were not for you, I doubt I would even be standing here. No—I know that I wouldn't be here. I wouldn't even be alive."

Stunned, Jack looked at him and asked, "What are you talking about?"

"I grew up in a dysfunctional family," Joey said. "My father, manically abusive, left my mother with three children. We never saw him again. I was the oldest of the three. And though I often caught the brunt of his abuse, I still felt something lacking in my life without him there. Meanwhile, my mother struggled to make ends meet, and she was always stressed and out of sorts. Home life was miserable. I was struggling with drugs and alcohol, and I was on the verge of dropping out of school. The thing was; I really didn't care. In fact, I didn't care about much of anything. I was constantly depressed. From the time I was 15, barely a day went by when I wasn't thinking about suicide. I was a mess.

"Then, well, a whole train of bad things happened to me, and I just couldn't take it anymore. I wished I were dead, and finally decided to go ahead and kill myself. I really meant it this time. I went to a hardware store after school and bought a rope and threw it in my backpack and headed home. I was determined to hang myself in my room so that my mother would walk in and be the first to see me dead."

"Ouch," Jack said, listening in rapt attention.

"Well," Joey continued, "here is where you come in. I don't even know if you remember, but I was walking home, past the school, and you came up to me and, just very kindly, said, 'Hi, Joey. How are you?' I didn't even think that you knew who I was, much less my name. But we chatted, and you invited me over to your house. We hung out in your room for a couple of hours, playing video games. You probably don't even remember any of this, do you?"

Jack kind of shrugged. "Well ... I think, well, I do ... but, well, vaguely, maybe."

"It doesn't matter. What matters is that my mood completely changed that day. I walked out of your house, threw the rope into the first dumpster I came to, and moved on. I never again contemplated suicide. Can't say my life has been great, but things have gotten better for me. The thing is, I always wanted to thank you for the kindness you showed me that day. It saved my life."

We might not all be suicidal teenagers, but we are flesh and blood, and even more so we are all emotional creatures. Our emotions easily drive us to action even more than our reason does.

Think back to a time someone did something kind for you. You haven't forgotten about it, have you?

Now think back to a time someone was unkind to you. You haven't forgotten about that, either, have you?

Now think about a time, if you can, when you were kind to someone, just for the sake of being kind. You weren't trying to get something from them. You were just being kind for the sake of being kind. How did that kindness make you feel?

Everyone has heard of the Golden Rule, "Do unto others as you would have them do to you."

What kind of world would we live in if everybody lived that way? Wars and crime would be finished. There would be no such thing as child prostitution or rape or drug wars. We could leave our doors unlocked. No one would be cold or hungry. Imagine raising your kids in that kind of world.

I read a magazine article in which the author stated that he had spent years interviewing famous people. People who had made it. These people had everything the world could offer them, and they kept it all for themselves. And yet, he found that most of these people were utterly miserable. They were some of the most dissatisfied, unhappy people he had ever met.

At the height of their success, Beatle Paul McCarthy said, "We've been the Beatles, which was marvelous...but I think generally there was this feeling of 'Yeah, well, it's great to be famous, it's great to be rich—but what's it all for?"

John Lennon, another Beatle, said this, "You're born in pain, and pain is what we're in most of the time."

Pretty interesting statements from men who had what most of us can only dream about. Great riches and worldwide fame wasn't enough. It didn't bring meaning and happiness to their lives.

Medieval writer Machiavelli apparently knew what he was talking about when he said, "Don't you know how little pleasure a man gets from the things he desires compared to what he hoped to find?"

The magazine writer mentioned earlier who interviewed famous people, also interviewed people who had dedicated their lives to the service of others. These were people whose whole lives were centered not on themselves but on giving to others, to reaching out and showing kindness and compassion to the needy. The contrast was striking. Those who were living in kindness for the benefit of others, rather than just for themselves, were much happier, much more fulfilled than those who lived only for themselves.

Perhaps it is counterintuitive, but it would seem to be that those who are kind, loving and follow the Golden Rule live happier lives.

The ancient Greeks told a story, called the Myth of Gyges, a farmer who was working in the fields when an earthquake struck. The ground opened up and he saw a statute that had been buried. He noticed there was a beautiful ring on the hand of the statue. Hey, why not? he thought, as he jumped in, grabbed the ring, and jumped out again just as the ground closed up. He put the ring on his finger, held it up to the sun, and greatly admired his new piece of adornment. A few weeks later, Gyges was in town, in a room, with a group of other people when he noticed something truly odd. When he turned the top of the ring a certain way—he disappeared. Just vanished. The people in the room were saying, "Where is Gyges? What happened to him?" He then saw that, when he turned the top of the ring the other way, he reappeared. Gyges realized that the ring afforded him great power, and he used that power to murder the king, rape the queen, and take control of the kingdom.

The point of the story was to show what people would do if they had absolute power and knew that no one could stop them. It's not a particularly positive commentary on the human condition.

But human history is filled with examples of what people would do to others if they could, and that they would not typically be kind. Too bad—because in so many ways, kindness is not that hard.

Quintus Fabius Maximus, known to history simply as Fabius, was a great Roman leader and general. These leaders demanded absolute loyalty from their troops. Roman tradition, the kind of tradition that made this small nation in Italy the ruler of the ancient world, demanded that soldiers obey their commanders or receive severe punishment, no questions asked.

A Roman soldier named Marsian had been speaking against Fabius, undermining his command and urging soldiers to desert. Word of Marsian's treachery and insubordination got back to Fabius and he ordered Marsian to be brought before him. Fabius then confronted Marsian, told him he knew what he had been doing and reminded him of the seriousness of his actions. But instead of punishing Marsian, he told him that he was to come directly back to him with any complaints.

Quintus Fabius Maximus

"Come to me personally, with your issues and I will look at them," he told the soldier. Then he gave Marsian an excellent horse and other gifts. As a result of Fabius' mercy to Marsian, he became the most trustworthy and faithful soldier in the entire army.

Fabius was merciful when he could have been harsh. He was kind when he could have been cruel. Kind when he could have been stern and hard and demanding. Look at the power it unleashed. He won the man's heart—and the rest of the man followed.

Kindness creates loyalty.

Another important aspect of kindness is appreciativeness. People want to be appreciated, noticed, and recognized. Appreciation creates value. I believe that each person has a deep craving to be appreciated. People want to be noticed and recognized. Appreciation tells the individual that they have worth, and each of us has something to give that no one else has.

Not long ago, an airplane on short hop from San Diego to Los Angeles suddenly began to pitch and shake and lose altitude. The pilot radioed the tower saying they were in deep trouble and might not make it. In a desperate move, he had the flight attendant move the passengers to the front of the plane in an effort to shift the weight and bring the nose down. It worked, at least enough to eventually get the plane to land safely.

It was a close call, closer than most realized.

As the passengers disembarked, one of them handed a flight attendant a note, saying: "You guys monkeying around up there in the cockpit have now caused me to miss my connection!"

A simple thank you might have sufficed.

Show appreciation. It requires a minimum of effort and can make a tremendous difference.

Many years ago, President Jimmy Carter said, "Life isn't fair." And it isn't.

It's not fair that some people can afford to drink from a $10,000 bottle of champagne, while billions around the world drink only filthy, terribly polluted water. While you may not be drinking expensive champagne, you have privileges over others in this world. And for that, be thankful.

But, the question is, What can we do about the unfairness of life? It's unrealistic to think we can eradicate injustice and create a world that is fair to everyone, but we can do our part. We can change our little part of the world.

You may have seen the movie The Blind Side, starring Sandra Bullock. It was about a wealthy family in Memphis who took in a troubled inner city youth. Michael Oher, the young man who became part of their family, went on to play in the NFL.

In one scene, Bullock was sitting in a restaurant with a bunch of her rich, well-heeled friends. They couldn't imagine how she could take a kid off the street and let him live in her home, pay for his education, and make him one of the family. Bullock's character answered that while the young man was benefiting greatly from their generosity, she and her family were benefiting even more. Being kind, being generous, even if you have just a little to give, can be one of the most rewarding things you can do.

When a powerful hand has a soft touch as its first instinct, it is called gentleness. It is the power of personal restraint when the injury of another is looming or imminent from your own hand. It is restraint actuated by a desire for the good of another.

Think about that for a minute.

A German woman lived through World War II. Life had been hard. She and her family had struggled mightily to survive. Living in what was then Czechoslovakia, she never thought of herself as being anti-Semitic. In fact, she had never even known a Jewish person really. And yet, motivated by fear, she did what the Nazi leaders told her to do. This was the case with many good people during those terrible days.

The woman remembered standing in the window of her apartment one day and hearing a ruckus outside. Looking out she saw a group of German soldiers, the feared SS, herding Jews through the street, men, women, and children. It was freezing outside, and yet these Jews weren't even wearing shoes. She watched as they huddled against a wall, crying and wailing and shaking in fear.

She remembers that she looked out at them and felt no sympathy for them at all. Her heart felt dead. She didn't hate them or wish them ill. In fact, she had no feeling for them one way or another. In later years, she said that she thought her reaction was inhuman. She said that for the first time in her life, she felt that, "I wasn't human."

Most of us have an innate sympathy, especially for those we care about and often even for those we don't know personally. But have you ever felt sympathy for someone you don't like?

A story from the Civil War tells of a man who traveled for days on horseback to find General Ulysses S. Grant. He asked to see the general and was finally allowed into the presence of the great man. He stated his name and his mission: to plead for the life of Frederick Stone, a soldier who was to be executed for the crime of desertion. Grant responded by saying that just because he came to plead for the life of a great friend, he wasn't going to commute the death sentence.

"A great friend?" the man responded. "I have no greater enemy than Frederick Stone."

Grant, stunned, hesitated for a few moments and then said, "You would come all this way for, not your friend, but for your enemy? Am I hearing that correctly?"

"Yes, sir, you are," he responded.

Grant looked at him and said: "For a man who would ride four days in dangerous territory, all to plead the life of an enemy…I will grant the request."

Being kind to those who we love is the right thing, the easy thing to do. But to show kindness to those who we feel don't deserve it is something special. Are you willing to do that? If so, you are sure to be blessed in ways you can't imagine.

Another important aspect of kindness is gratitude. When someone says the words, "good character," one of the first qualities that comes to mind is a very simple one—kindness.

Ulysses S. Grant

Here are some specific ways you can give kindness to others:

• Show mercy by forgiving people when they don't deserve it and stay loyal even when things get difficult (use common sense—don't pledge loyalty to a "Hitler").

• Give people benevolence and undeserved kindness even when you get nothing in return.

• Respond to other people's pain with compassion—even people you don't know well.

• Express appreciation. Everyone needs to be appreciated, noticed, and recognized.

• Be thankful, really thankful, for what you have.

• Be fair.

• Be generous. The act of giving is more of a gift than the gift itself. Go ahead—ponder that for a minute.

• Be gentle. Control your strength with love.

• Be sympathetic. Allow yourself to by someone else's situation. It's what makes you human.

• Become patient. It's a process.

• Look for deeper understanding. Get over yourself and put yourself in someone else's shoes.

• Strip off your pride and wear humility. It looks better on you.

• Defer to others. Give other people a chance to learn from their mistakes, too.

• Be cheerful. It's not that difficult. And it's contagious.

• Peace out—in other words, choose to live in peace with others and peace with yourself.

Read through these scriptures

1 Corinthians 13:4 "Charity suffereth long, [and] is kind; charity envieth not; charity vaunteth not itself, is not puffed up…."

Ephesians 4:32 "And be ye kind one to another, tenderhearted, forgiving one another, even as God for Christ's sake hath forgiven you."

Colossians 3:12 "Put on therefore, as the elect of God, holy and beloved, bowels of mercies, kindness, humbleness of mind, meekness, longsuffering;"

1 Peter 3:8 "Finally, [be ye] all of one mind, having compassion one of another, love as brethren, [be] pitiful, [be] courteous:"

1 John 3:17 "But whoso hath this world's good, and seeth his brother have need, and shutteth up his bowels [of compassion] from him, how dwelleth the love of God in him?"

Jude 1:22 "And of some have compassion, making a difference:"

Think through and check the box that fits what you think

1. The Christian is to have an atmosphere surrounding his soul that shall be full of pleasantness, courtesy, and kindness, and represent the Spirit of Christ. These qualities of character are to be perseveringly cherished, and employed in the work of God, giving character to that work in representing Christ to the world.

1) ☐ strongly agree   2) ☐ agree   3) ☐ neutral   4) ☐ disagree   5) ☐ strongly disagree

2. We must cherish kindness.

1) ☐ strongly agree   2) ☐ agree   3) ☐ neutral   4) ☐ disagree   5) ☐ strongly disagree

3. The disposition to leave deeds of kindness undone is a manifest weakness and defect in your character.

1) ☐ strongly agree   2) ☐ agree   3) ☐ neutral   4) ☐ disagree   5) ☐ strongly disagree

4. The faces of men and women who talk with God, to whom the invisible world is a reality, express the peace of God. They carry with them the soft and genial atmosphere of heaven, and diffuse it in deeds of kindness and works of love. Their influence is of a character to win souls to Christ.

1) ☐ strongly agree   2) ☐ agree   3) ☐ neutral   4) ☐ disagree   5) ☐ strongly disagree

5. You cannot be like Jesus, and cherish pride in your heart.

1) ☐ strongly agree   2) ☐ agree   3) ☐ neutral   4) ☐ disagree   5) ☐ strongly disagree

6. You cannot give place to envy or jealousy be like the Character of Jesus.

1) ☐ strongly agree   2) ☐ agree   3) ☐ neutral   4) ☐ disagree   5) ☐ strongly disagree

7. You must consider it beneath the character of a Christian to harbor resentful thoughts or indulge in recrimination.

1) ☐ strongly agree   2) ☐ agree   3) ☐ neutral   4) ☐ disagree   5) ☐ strongly disagree

8. Never comment upon the character or the acts of others in a manner to injure them.

1) ☐ strongly agree   2) ☐ agree   3) ☐ neutral   4) ☐ disagree   5) ☐ strongly disagree

9. In no case make their failures or defects the subject of ridicule or unkind criticism.

1) ☐ strongly agree   2) ☐ agree   3) ☐ neutral   4) ☐ disagree   5) ☐ strongly disagree

10. You lessen your own influence by so doing, and lead others to doubt your sincerity as a Christian.

1) ☐ strongly agree   2) ☐ agree   3) ☐ neutral   4) ☐ disagree   5) ☐ strongly disagree

11. Let peace and love dwell in your soul, and ever cherish a forgiving spirit.

1) ☐ strongly agree   2) ☐ agree   3) ☐ neutral   4) ☐ disagree   5) ☐ strongly disagree

Highlight thoughts below that expresses what you believe

Humanity must be touched with the sufferings of humanity, that men and women might learn how to show tenderness, kindness, and pity, and thus a Christ-likeness of character be developed in humanity. In this way they were to be fitted to be missionaries. This is the work that is to be done everywhere. *SS.1896-01-01.002*

In the strength of Him whose loving-kindness is exercised toward the helpless, the ignorant, and those counted as the least of His little ones, we must labor for their future welfare, for the shaping of Christian character. The very ones who need help the most will at times try our patience sorely. "Take heed that ye despise not one of these little ones," Christ says, "for I say unto you, That in heaven their angels do always behold the face of My Father which is in heaven." Matthew 18:10. And to those who minister to these souls, the Saviour declares: "Inasmuch as ye have done it unto one of the least of these My brethren, ye have done it unto Me." Matthew 25:40. *6T.348.003*

If the radiance of His Spirit is reflected from you in a Christlike character, if sympathy, kindness, forbearance, and love are abiding principles in your life, you will be a blessing to all around you. You will not criticize others or manifest a harsh, denunciatory spirit toward them; you will not feel that their ideas must be made to meet your standard; but the love of Jesus and the peaceable fruits of righteousness will be revealed in you. *5T.650.001*

We..."should possess the attributes of Christ's character--patience, kindness, mercy, and love; and into the daily experience they should bring the Saviour's righteousness and peace. Then, working with fragrant influence, they will give evidence of what grace can do through human agents who make God their trust. *CT.151.001*

God wants children to be lovely, not with artificial adornment, but with beauty of character, the charms of kindness and affection, which will make their hearts bound with joy and happiness. *HR.1877-09-01.009*

The lives of those who are connected with God are fragrant with deeds of love and goodness. The sweet savor of Christ surrounds them; their influence is to elevate and bless. These are fruitful trees. Men and women of this stamp of character will render practical service in thoughtful deeds of kindness, and earnest, systematic labor. *RH.1879-01-02.005*

We are not to trust in our own wisdom, but in the wisdom of God. This will bring into the character the patience, kindness, and love of Christ. *ST.1905-06-21.007*

How to be more kind:

1. Learn and teach what you understand kindness to be.

2. Encourage and celebrate kindness whenever and wherever you see it.

3. In this age of Twitter and Facebook, collect, share and initiate acts of kindness.

4. Applaud and affirm acts of kindness.

5. Accept and integrate kindness as God's 24/7 divine design for your own mind, thoughts and actions.

6. Practice kindness through micro (meaning little) choices and actions and macro (meaning ig) choices and actions you perform every day

CHAPTER 8

LOVE

n the state of New York, there is an old cemetery that holds the graves of northern soldiers who fought and died during the Civil War. Over one grave in particular hangs the simple but touching epitaph, "He died for me."

The sign was placed there by a man who had been drafted to fight in that war, the bloodiest in American history. He had a wife and children and despaired at the thought of leaving them alone and unprotected in the event of his death.

As he prepared for his departure, someone knocked on the door. The man opened the door to find a stranger. "I have neither a wife nor a child," the young man said. "You have a family, so I've arranged to go in your place."

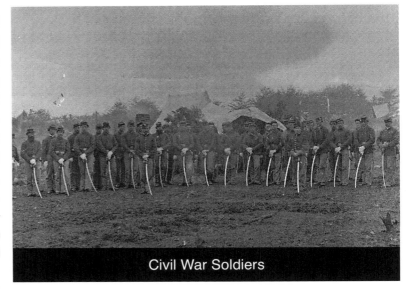

Civil War Soldiers

Throughout the many months of that terrible war, this father watched the newspaper for a list of the wounded and dead. One day he saw the young man's name and noted that he had died on a nearby battlefield. The man rushed to retrieve the body. Having identified the young man among the fallen, the man brought his body home. There with great tenderness and respect, he buried the young man in his family cemetery, and attached the sign saying, "He died for me."

What would cause someone to give his life for another as the young man in this story did? Love—the highest and most noble expression of character. It's the only explanation for such a pure and selfless sacrifice on behalf of a stranger and it is the eighth secret to a better life.

For our purposes, we will examine three forms of love: Eros, which is the Greek word for romantic love; Philos, which is the Greek word for brotherly love; and Agape, which is the Greek word for the purest and most noble form of love.

Eros—the kind of love that inspires poets, and splits kingdoms, and binds the hearts of lovers old and young.

Sure, that sounds a little dramatic, but anyone who has ever experienced the euphoria of eros won't deny that it's true.

We hadn't dated for very long before I knew I was madly in love with this pretty girl. Everything took on an enhanced meaning. Every song seemed to be about us. The campus was more beautiful, classes were more exciting, and no matter what I was doing, a part of me was always thinking about Linda. Love also makes you do stupid things.

Now, I'm not a plumber. But I am observant and determined, so when one of the faucets at Linda's mother's house stopped working, I saw this as an opportunity to gain some manly points. I'm still not sure exactly how I did it—we'll call it a mix of desperation and perseverance—but I fixed it! Linda called me her "knight in shining armor," and every day since then I've been determined to keep that image alive. Linda and I were married, and we still enjoy telling people we met on "a trip around the world." That feeling of being in love with my wife—I have it to this day.

But I meet so many husbands and wives who have become little more than roommates. That eros has dwindled from flames to burning coals, and then to ashes. Their marriages are cold. I heard about a couple that was driving home from a restaurant where they had celebrated their twenty-fifth wedding anniversary. Sitting over against the door, the wife began to reminisce. "Oh, honey, remember when we were so close? When we first got married, we sat so close that you could hardly shift the gears, and look at us now!"

Her husband quickly responded, "I do remember, but I'm not the one who moved!"

Maintaining a marriage requires the hard work of learning to love each other in more and better ways. It requires learning to make the decision that your love is more important than hurt feelings. It requires making all of the other aspects of your life subservient to the preservation of that relationship. It requires opening your heart over and over and over again.

It reminds me of a couple that had been married for fifty years. One day the wife said to her husband, "Things have changed. You use to sit very close to me."

"Well, I can remedy that," the husband answered. He got up and moved over next to her on the sofa.

"You also used to hold me tight," said the wife. "Do you remember?"

"Yes, I do," answered the husband. He placed his arms around her and gave her a big hug. Then he asked, "How's that?"

With a little smile on her face, the wife continued, "You used to nuzzle my neck and nibble on my ear. Do you remember that?"

All of a sudden the husband jumped to his feet and left the room.

"Where are you going?" his wife called after him.

"I'll be right back," he answered. "I've got to get my teeth!"

Romantic love is a wonderful thing if you do it right.

You would not leave a beautiful diamond lying around where it could be lost or stolen. You take good care of your home and your car. You guard your health by disciplining yourself to eat well and exercise. In the same way, when you are given the gift of romantic love, you have to guard what you've received. And sometimes it's the simple things that can keep love alive. Holding hands, soft kisses, special songs. The things you did without thinking when you were first in love.

Possibly the most important component to marriage is purity. Without a commitment to monogamy, it's possible to lose something you can never get back. Society today urges us to gratify ourselves in the moment, but the beauty and sacred nature of genuine, long-lasting romantic love comes as the result of respect, faithfulness and commitment. Those who sell out in the heat of the moment lose out in the end. Only those who have kept the purity of their love intact are blessed to experience the joy and completeness it brings.

Philos, the second type of love, is the love you might feel for a friend or a sibling. It also creates a strong, compelling bond.

The real work begins the moment you close this Study Guide. Living out the principles in this book takes courage. Everything that's worth doing does—and that's why I want to leave you with a story of encouragement as you prepare to begin the journey ahead of you.

Richard Lee Norris was a good-looking guy in his early 20s with a future full of possibilities. One day, all of that changed. Norris noticed his shotgun was in its case, leaning up against the glass window. He unlocked the case and reached down to move it off of the glass, when it suddenly discharged in his face.

When the gun fired, it took off his jaw, his lips and his nose. He was left with a small amount of protection for his eyes and a little bit of tongue. Though he survived the incident, he was horribly disfigured, and spent his time as a recluse, hiding behind a mask whenever he had to go out in public—even choosing to shop late at night so there would be fewer people to stare or point at his appearance.

Fifteen years later, a young man named Joshua in Maryland was crossing a street, not realizing the arrow for turning traffic was green. He was struck, and clung feebly to life while the University of Maryland Shock Trauma Unit worked to save him. Despite their skilled efforts, Joshua died.

Joshua's family decided to donate his organs. In the midst of their tragic loss, the family gave away the precious, life-giving pieces of their son. One of the brave decisions the family made was to donate Joshua's face and jaw to Richard Lee Norris.

Richard Lee Norris was the recipient of the most extensive face plant ever done in history. When he healed from the surgery, he had a new face, a new jaw, and a new chance at a normal life.

While we don't all experience the kind of trauma Richard Lee Norris dealt with, we've all been wounded. We all have reasons to hide. But just like Norris, we have the opportunity at a new life—a new chance to rebuild what we've been given, start over, and start living life that is truly life. Regardless of the ways you have been damaged, or treated with injustice, or the number of missed opportunities in your rearview mirror, you now have the chance to become the person you were always meant to be. You can heal and change, and in turn, help others in the healing and changing process. Don't quit. Come out, come out wherever you are.

Love Is the Greatest

Read through these scriptures

1 Corinthians 13 "If I could speak all the languages of earth and of angels, but didn't love others, I would only be a noisy gong or a clanging cymbal. 2 If I had the gift of prophecy, and if I understood all of God's secret plans and possessed all knowledge, and if I had such faith that I could move mountains, but didn't love others, I would be nothing. 3 If I gave everything I have to the poor and even sacrificed my body, I could boast about it;[a] but if I didn't love others, I would have gained nothing.

⁴ Love is patient and kind. Love is not jealous or boastful or proud 5 or rude. It does not demand its own way. It is not irritable, and it keeps no record of being wronged. 6 It does not rejoice about injustice but rejoices whenever the truth wins out. 7 Love never gives up, never loses faith, is always hopeful, and endures through every circumstance.

⁸ Prophecy and speaking in unknown languages[b] and special knowledge will become useless. But love will last forever! 9 Now our knowledge is partial and incomplete, and even the gift of prophecy reveals only part of the whole picture! 10 But when the time of perfection comes, these partial things will become useless.

¹¹ When I was a child, I spoke and thought and reasoned as a child. But when I grew up, I put away childish things. 12 Now we see things imperfectly, like puzzling reflections in a mirror, but then we will see everything with perfect clarity.[c] All that I know now is partial and incomplete, but then I will know everything completely, just as God now knows me completely.

¹³ Three things will last forever—faith, hope, and love—and the greatest of these is love."

Matthew 5:43" Ye have heard that it hath been said, Thou shalt love thy neighbour, and hate thine enemy."

Matthew 5:44 "But I say unto you, Love your enemies, bless them that curse you, do good to them that hate you, and pray for them which despitefully use you, and persecute you;"

Matthew 5:46 "For if ye love them which love you, what reward have ye? do not even the publicans the same?"

Matthew 22:37 "Jesus said unto him, Thou shalt love the Lord thy God with all thy heart, and with all thy soul, and with all thy mind."

Matthew 22:38 "This is the first and great commandment."

Matthew 22:39 "And the second [is] like unto it, Thou shalt love thy neighbour as thyself."

Luke 6:27 "But I say unto you which hear, Love your enemies, do good to them which hate you,"

Romans 12:9 "[Let] love be without dissimulation. Abhor that which is evil; cleave to that which is good."

Romans 12:10 "[Be] kindly affectioned one to another with brotherly love; in honour preferring one another;"

Romans 13:8 "Owe no man anything, but to love one another: for he that loveth another hath fulfilled the law.

Romans 13:10 "Love worketh no ill to his neighbour: therefore love [is] the fulfilling of the law."

1 Corinthians 2:9 "But as it is written, Eye hath not seen, nor ear heard, neither have entered into the heart of man, the things which God hath prepared for them that love him."

Galatians 5:14 "For all the law is fulfilled in one word, [even] in this; Thou shalt love thy neighbour as thyself."

Philippians 2:1 "If [there be] therefore any consolation in Christ, if any comfort of love, if any fellowship of the Spirit, if any bowels and mercies,"

Philippians 2:2 Fulfil ye my joy, that ye be likeminded, having the same love, [being] of one accord, of one mind."

1 Thessalonians 4:9 "But as touching brotherly love ye need not that I write unto you: for ye yourselves are taught of God to love one another."

Hebrews 10:24 "And let us consider one another to provoke unto love and to good works:"

1 Peter 2:17 "Honour all [men]. Love the brotherhood. Fear God. Honour the king."

1 John 2:5 "But whoso keepeth his word, in him verily is the love of God perfected: hereby know we that we are in him."

1 John 3:11 "For this is the message that ye heard from the beginning, that we should love one another."

1 John 3:14 "We know that we have passed from death unto life, because we love the brethren. He that loveth not [his] brother abideth in death."

1. John 4:7 "Beloved, let us love one another: for love is of God; and every one that loveth is born of God, and knoweth God."

1. John 4:8 "He that loveth not knoweth not God; for God is love."

1. John 4:9 "In this was manifested the love of God toward us, because that God sent his only begotten Son into the world, that we might live through him."

1. John 4:10 "Herein is love, not that we loved God, but that he loved us, and sent his Son [to be] the propitiation for our sins."

1. John 4:11 "Beloved, if God so loved us, we ought also to love one another."

1. John 4:12 "No man hath seen God at any time. If we love one another, God dwelleth in us, and his love is perfected in us."

1. John 4:17 "Herein is our love made perfect, that we may have boldness in the day of judgment: because as he is, so are we in this world."

1. John 4:18 "There is no fear in love; but perfect love casteth out fear: because fear hath torment. He that feareth is not made perfect in love."

1. John 4:19 "We love him, because he first loved us."

Think through and check the box that fits what you think

1. The more closely we resemble our Saviour in character the greater will be our love toward those for whom He died.

1) ☐ strongly agree   2) ☐ agree   3) ☐ neutral   4) ☐ disagree   5) ☐ strongly disagree

2. We are to manifest forth to the world His character cherishing that tender love one for another that will bear to the world the credentials of the power of Christ to link heart to heart in the strongest bands of fellowship and brotherhood.

1) ☐ strongly agree   2) ☐ agree   3) ☐ neutral   4) ☐ disagree   5) ☐ strongly disagree

3. Christ's favorite theme was the paternal character and abundant love of God. This knowledge of God was Christ's own gift to men, and this gift He has committed to His people to be communicated by them to the world.

1) ☐ strongly agree   2) ☐ agree   3) ☐ neutral   4) ☐ disagree   5) ☐ strongly disagree

4. We are to be distinguished from the world because God has placed His seal upon us, because He manifests in us His own character of love.

1) ☐ strongly agree   2) ☐ agree   3) ☐ neutral   4) ☐ disagree   5) ☐ strongly disagree

5. As they continue to follow Jesus, they will become more like him in character. Love to God and man will pervade the life.

1) ☐ strongly agree   2) ☐ agree   3) ☐ neutral   4) ☐ disagree   5) ☐ strongly disagree

6. It is the pure in heart who shall see God, in His true character as a God of love. He who has

the love of God (shed, shared?) abroad in his heart, will reflect the purity and love which exists in Jehovah, and which Christ represented in our world.

1) ☐ strongly agree   2) ☐ agree   3) ☐ neutral   4) ☐ disagree   5) ☐ strongly disagree

7. The qualities that it are essential for all to possess in order to know God are those that mark the completeness of Christ's character: His love, His patience, His unselfishness.

1) ☐ strongly agree   2) ☐ agree   3) ☐ neutral   4) ☐ disagree   5) ☐ strongly disagree

8. Justice has a twin sister – Love, and they should stand side by side.

1) ☐ strongly agree   2) ☐ agree   3) ☐ neutral   4) ☐ disagree   5) ☐ strongly disagree

9. Those who believe in Christ possess the character of Christ, have the love of Christ, [and] are one with Him.

1) ☐ strongly agree   2) ☐ agree   3) ☐ neutral   4) ☐ disagree   5) ☐ strongly disagree

10. You must be doers of the word, and possess that love that was manifested in the life and character of Christ. "

1) ☐ strongly agree   2) ☐ agree   3) ☐ neutral   4) ☐ disagree   5) ☐ strongly disagree

11. Will it make us miserable to follow this plan of Christian progression?-- No. It will bring heaven nearer to us. We may have the sweet peace and consolation of God in doing this work. These steps will take us into the atmosphere of heaven; for as God sees his children seeking to carry out his instruction in their habits and thoughts, he multiplies grace, and gives them that wisdom that cometh down from above, that is "first pure, then peaceable, gentle, and easy to be entreated, full of mercy and good fruits."

1) ☐ strongly agree   2) ☐ agree   3) ☐ neutral   4) ☐ disagree   5) ☐ strongly disagree

12. "Wherefore the rather, brethren, give diligence to make your calling and election sure; for if ye do these things, ye shall never fall."

1) ☐ strongly agree   2) ☐ agree   3) ☐ neutral   4) ☐ disagree   5) ☐ strongly disagree

Highlight thoughts below that expresses what you believe

We are continually to behold him, to meditate on the grace of his CHARACTER to contemplate his love; and by beholding, we shall become changed. *RH.1891-06-30.011*

Jesus revealed to the world, in his character that "God is love." The beloved apostle exclaims, "Behold what manner of love the Father hath bestowed upon us, that we should be called the sons of God! therefore the world knoweth us not, because it knew him not. Beloved, now are we the sons of God, and it doth not yet appear what we shall be: but we know that, when he shall appear, we shall be like him; for we shall see him as he is." *YI.1894-07-26.006*

God has placed His seal upon us, because He manifests in us His own character of love. *7T.144.002*

Christ is seeking to uplift all who will be lifted to companionship with Himself, that we may be one with Him as He is one with the Father. He permits us to come in contact with suffering and calamity in order to call us out of our selfishness; He seeks to develop in us the attributes of His character--compassion, tenderness, and love. *COL.389.001*

Those who wait for the Bridegroom's coming are to say to the people, "Behold your God." The last rays of merciful light, the last message of mercy to be given to the world, is a revelation of His character of love. The children of God are to manifest His glory. In their own life and character they are to reveal what the grace of God has done for them. COL.416.001

Christ, the Word, the revelation of God,--the manifestation of His character, His law, His love, His life,--is the only foundation upon which we can build a character that will endure. We build on Christ by obeying His word. *MB.149.001*

If we are partakers of his divine nature, we shall have his mind, and represent his character in deeds of love and mercy toward others. *HM.1894-12-01.003*

Faith in Christ, expressed in the life and character, revealed in love for God and for our brethren, makes the human agent a power in the world and in the church. *LU.1909-11-17.011*

The elevation of man is the object of the plan of salvation. This elevation of character is to be reached through the merit and grace of Christ. We are continually to behold him, to meditate on the grace of his character, to contemplate his love; and by beholding, we shall become changed. *RH.1891-06-30.011*

When we have a sense of what God is, we shall realize our own unworthiness; but we shall also have confidence toward God, knowing what is his character of mercy and love. We shall come into his presence through the merits of Christ, and through him have boldness and confidence. We may plead the promises of God without the fear of being presumptuous. *RH.1895-05-28.009*

....His character is love. " *RH.1899-10-10.009*

The Lord permits suffering and calamity to come upon men and women to call us out of our selfishness, to awaken in us the attributes of his character,--compassion, tenderness, and love. *RH.1899-10-10.013*

Sanctification of the soul, body, and spirit is the sure result of this union with Christ. What is the character of the fruit?--Love, joy, peace, long-suffering, gentleness, goodness, faith, meekness, temperance. Wherever there is union with Christ, there is love. *ST.1891-08-10.004*

The love of Jesus with its redeeming power has come into the heart to conquer the entire being, body, soul, and spirit. When counter-influences work to oppose the grace of Christ which bringeth salvation, this love masters every other motive, and raises the human being above the corrupting influences of the world. *ST.1898-10-13.006*

Christ loves His church. He will give all needed help to those who call upon Him for strength for the development of Christlike character. But His love is not weakness. ST.1901-11-13.008

The qualities that it is essential for all to possess in order to know God are those that mark the completeness of Christ's character,--his love, his patience, his unselfishness. These attributes are cultivated by doing kind actions with a kindly heart. *YI.1900-03-22.007*

This world needs your reflection of God's Perfection. So keep your eyes fixed on the person you would like to be—the person who is always ready when destiny calls, to resemble reflect and reveal the Character of Christ.

2. Corinthians 7:1 Having therefore these promises, dearly beloved, let us cleanse ourselves from all filthiness of the flesh and spirit, perfecting holiness in the fear of God. *2 Corinthians 7:1 (NLT)*

[1] Because we have these promises, dear friends, let us cleanse ourselves from everything that can defile our body or spirit. And let us work toward complete holiness because we fear God.

Ephesians 4:12 For the perfecting of the saints, for the work of the ministry, for the edifying of the body of Christ: *Ephesians 4:12 (NLT)*

[12] Their responsibility is to equip God's people to do his work and build up the church, the body of Christ.

"Every day, as I surrender to God and cooperate with God, He is perfecting me."

READ THROUGH THESE SCRIPTURES

Genesis 17:1 "and when Abram was ninety years old and nine, the Lord appeared to Abram, and said unto him, I [am] the almighty God; walk before me, and be thou perfect." *Genesis 17:1 (NLT)*

¹ "When Abram was ninety-nine years old, the LORD appeared to him and said, "I am El-Shadd-ai—'God Almighty.' Serve Me faithfully and live a blameless life."

Deuteronomy 18:13 "Thou shalt be perfect with the Lord thy God." *Deuteronomy 18:12-13 (NLT)*

¹³ "But you must be blameless before the LORD your God."

2 Samuel 22:33 "God [is] my strength [and] power: and He maketh my way perfect." *2 Samuel 22:33 (NLT)*

³³ "God is my strong fortress, and he makes my way perfect. "

1 Kings 8:61 "let your heart therefore be perfect with the lord our God, to walk in his statutes, and to keep His commandments, as at this day." *1 Kings 8:60-61 (NLT)*

⁶⁰ "Then people all over the earth will know that the LORD alone is God and there is no other."

⁶¹ "And may you be completely faithful to the LORD our God. May you always obey His decrees and commands, just as you are doing today."

2 Chronicles 16:9 "For the eyes of the Lord run to and fro throughout the whole earth, to show Himself strong in the behalf of [them] whose heart [is] perfect toward Him." *2 Chronicles 16:9 (NLT)*

⁹ "The eyes of the LORD search the whole earth in order to strengthen those whose hearts are fully committed to Him. What a fool you have been! From now on you will be at war."

Job 1:1 "There was a man in the land of Uz, whose name [was] Job; and that man was perfect and upright, and one that feared God, and eschewed evil." *Job 1:1 (NLT)*

¹ "There once was a man named Job who lived in the land of Uz. He was blameless—a man of complete integrity. He feared God and stayed away from evil."

Job 1:8 "And the Lord said unto Satan, hast thou considered my servant Job, that [there is] none like him in the earth, a perfect and an upright man, one that feareth God, and escheweth evil?" *Job 1:8 (NLT)*

⁸ "Then the LORD asked Satan, "Have you noticed my servant Job? He is the finest man in all the earth. He is blameless—a man of complete integrity. He fears God and stays away from evil."

Psalms 18:32 "[it is] God that girdeth me with strength, and maketh my way perfect." *Psalm 18:32 (NLT)*

³² "God arms me with strength, and He makes my way perfect."

Psalms 37:37 "Mark the perfect [man], and behold the upright: for the end of [that] man [is] peace."

Psalms 64:4 "That they may shoot in secret at the perfect: suddenly do they shoot at him, and fear not."

Psalms 64:7 "But God shall shoot at them [with] an arrow; suddenly shall they be wounded. *Psalm 64:4-8 (NLT)*

⁴ "They shoot from ambush at the innocent, attacking suddenly and fearlessly."

⁵ "They encourage each other to do evil and plan how to set their traps in secret. "Who will ever notice?" they ask."

⁶ "As they plot their crimes, they say, "We have devised the perfect plan!" Yes, the human heart and mind are cunning."

⁷ "But God Himself will shoot them with His arrows, suddenly striking them down."

⁸ "Their own tongues will ruin them, and all who see them will shake their heads in scorn."

Psalms 101:6 "Mine eyes [shall be] upon the faithful of the land, that they may dwell with me: he that walketh in a perfect way, he shall serve me." *Psalm 101:6 (NLT)*

⁶ "I will search for faithful people to be my companions. Only those who are above reproach will be allowed to serve me."

Ezekiel 28:15 "Thou [wast] perfect in thy ways from the day that thou wast created, till iniquity was found in thee."

2 Samuel 22:33 (NLT)

³³ "God is my strong fortress, and he makes my way perfect."

Psalm 18:32 (NLT)

³² "God arms me with strength, and he makes my way perfect."

Matthew 5:48 (NLT)

⁴⁸ "But you are to be perfect, even as your Father in heaven is perfect."

Matthew 19:21 (NLT)

²¹ "Jesus told him, "If you want to be perfect, go and sell all your possessions and give the money to the poor, and you will have treasure in heaven. Then come, follow me."

Colossians 1:28 (NLT)

²⁸ "So we tell others about Christ, warning everyone and teaching everyone with all the wisdom God has given us. We want to present them to God, perfect in their relationship to Christ."

Colossians 4:12 (NLT)

¹² "Epaphras, a member of your own fellowship and a servant of Christ Jesus, sends you his greetings. He always prays earnestly for you, asking God to make you strong and perfect, fully confident that you are following the whole will of God."

James 1:4 (NLT)

[4] "So let it grow, for when your endurance is fully developed, you will be perfect and complete, needing nothing."

James 3:2 (NLT)

[2] "Indeed, we all make many mistakes. For if we could control our tongues, we would be perfect and could also control ourselves in every other way."

---

1 John 4:17 (NLT)

[17] "And as we live in God, our love grows more perfect. So we will not be afraid on the day of judgment, but we can face him with confidence because we live like Jesus here in this world."

---

1 John 4:18 (NLT)

[18] "Such love has no fear, because perfect love expels all fear. If we are afraid, it is for fear of punishment, and this shows that we have not fully experienced his perfect love." Matthew 5:48 (NLT)

John 17:23 "I in them, and Thou in Me, that they may be made perfect in one; and that the world may know that Thou hast sent Me, and hast loved them, as thou hast loved Me."

Romans 12:2 "and be not conformed to this world: but be ye transformed by the renewing of your mind, that ye may prove what [is] that good, and acceptable, and perfect, will of God."

Romans 12:2 (NLT)

[2] "Don't copy the behavior and customs of this world, but let God transform you into a new person by changing the way you think. Then you will learn to know God's will for you, which is good and pleasing and perfect."

2 Corinthians 13:11: "Finally, brethren, farewell. Be perfect, be of good comfort, be of one mind, live in peace; and the God of love and peace shall be with you."

2 Corinthians 13:11 (NLT)

[11] "Dear brothers and sisters, I close my letter with these last words: Be joyful. Grow to maturity. Encourage each other. Live in harmony and peace. Then the God of love and peace will be with you."

Galatians 3:3 (NLT)

[3] "How foolish can you be? After starting your Christian lives in the Spirit, why are you now trying to become perfect by your own human effort?"

Ephesians 4:13: "Till we all come in the unity of the faith, and of the knowledge of the Son of God, unto a perfect man, unto the measure of the stature of the fullness of Christ:"

Ephesians 4:13 (NLT)

[13] "This will continue until we all come to such unity in our faith and knowledge of God's Son that we will be mature in the Lord, measuring up to the full and complete standard of Christ."

Colossians 1:28: "Whom we preach, warning every man, and teaching every man in all wisdom; that we may present every man perfect in Christ Jesus:"

Colossians 1:28-29 (NLT)

[28] "So we tell others about Christ, warning everyone and teaching everyone with all the wisdom God has given us. We want to present them to God, perfect in their relationship to Christ."

[29] "That's why I work and struggle so hard, depending on Christ's mighty power that works within me. "

2 Timothy 3:16 "All scripture [is] given by inspiration of God, and [is] profitable for doctrine, for reproof, for correction, for instruction in righteousness:"

2 Timothy 3:17 "That the man of God may be perfect, thoroughly furnished unto all good works."

2 Timothy 3:16-17 (NLT)

[16] "All Scripture is inspired by God and is useful to teach us what is true and to make us realize what is wrong in our lives. It corrects us when we are wrong and teaches us to do what is right."

[17] "God uses it to prepare and equip His people to do every good work."

Hebrews 2:10 (NLT)

[10] "God, for whom and through whom everything was made, chose to bring many children into glory. And it was only right that He should make Jesus, through His suffering, a perfect leader, fit to bring them into their salvation."

Hebrews 13:21 "Make you perfect in every good work to do His will, working in you that which is well pleasing in His sight, through Jesus Christ; to whom [be] glory for ever and ever. Amen."

Hebrews 13:21 (NLT)

[21] "May He equip you with all you need for doing His will. May He produce in you, through the power of Jesus Christ, every good thing that is pleasing to Him. All glory to Him forever and ever! Amen."

Hebrews 10:14 "For by one offering he hath perfected for ever them that are sanctified."

Hebrews 10:14 (NLT)

[14] "For by that one offering he forever made perfect those who are being made holy."

Hebrews 12:23 (NLT)

[23] "You have come to the assembly of God's firstborn children, whose names are written in heaven. You have come to God himself, who is the judge over all things. You have come to the spirits of the righteous ones in heaven who have now been made perfect."

INTRODUCTION
SC 64
SC.065.001
SC.065.002
ST.1893-04-17.011
SC.065.002
9T.021.002
9T.021.003
9T.022.002
9T.022.003
9T.023.001
RH.1890-12-09.004

FAITH AND BELIEF
5T.744.002
COL.112.005
COL.112.005
COL.310.004
H.1899-12-01.002
RH.1887-03-15.013
RH.1891-04-14.004
RH.1891-04-28.007
RH.1904-05-26.003
RH.1900-05-08.018
RH.1901-10-01.011
RH.1911-04-13.015
ST.1888-07-27.003
ST.1894-02-12.002
ST.1895-05-16.006
ST.1899-01-18.015
GC88.436.001
GW92.427.003

VIRTUE
RH.1888-02-21.004
MM.1893-10-01.005
RH.1888-02-21.004
RH.1905-08-31.006
ST.1885-10-15.008
AA.531.001

KNOWLEDGE
CED.065.001

8T.289.003
ED.195.002
MH.425.003
PK.693.002
PP.596.002
RH.1885-11-24.013
ST.1879-03-06.005
YI.1879-02-19.004
RH.1899-09-19.011
ST.1890-02-24.005
ST.1890-03-31.007

SELF CONTROL
AU.1907-04-29.005
PP.568.001
SL.023.002
HR.1878-11-01.005
RH.1884-06-10.011
RH.1907-10-31.006
YI.1884-01-30.002
YI.1907-11-12.008
SPM.264.001
GW92.421.001
2T.562.002
4T.361.001
PATIENCE
5T.307.001
CED.089.001
GC.094.003
RH.1894-01-16.008
RH.1897-11-30.009
RH.1899-01-03.017
LP.233.001

REVERENCE SACREDNESS
MB.149.002
3T.042.002
PP.307.001
ST.1886-11-18.013
SL.076.001
ST.1886-06-03.014
RH.1891-01-27.010
RH.1899-02-14.004

AU.1906-10-01.002
RH.1896-12-22.008
RH.1910-11-10.016
ST.1890-02-24.005

KINDNESS
SS.1896-01-01.002
6T.348.003
5T.650.001
CT.151.001
HR.1877-09-01.009
RH.1879-01-02.005
ST.1905-06-21.007

LOVE
RH.1891-06-30.011
YI.1894-07-26.006
7T.144.002
COL.389.001
COL.416.001
MB.149.001
HM.1894-12-01.003
LU.1909-11-17.011
RH.1891-06-30.011
RH.1895-05-28.009
RH.1899-10-10.009
RH.1899-10-10.013
ST.1891-08-10.004
ST.1898-10-13.006
ST.1901-11-13.008
YI.1900-03-22.007

EGW References

AA	Acts of the Apostles, The
AG	God's Amazing Grace
AH	Adventist Home, The
ApM	An Appeal to Mothers
AUCR	[Australasian] Union Conference Record
AY	Appeal to Youth
1BC	Bible Commentary, The SDA , Vol. 1 (2BC for Vol. 2, etc.)
BE	Bible Echo
1Bio	Biography of E. G. White, Vol. 1 (2Bio for Vol. 2, etc.)
BLJ	To Be Like Jesus
BTS	Bible Training School
CC	Conflict and Courage
CCh	Counsels for the Church
CD	Counsels on Diet and Foods
CE	Christian Education
CET	Christian Experience and Teaching
CEv	Colporteur Evangelist
CG	Child Guidance
CH	Counsels on Health
ChL	Christian Leadership
ChS	Christian Service
CL	Country Living
CM	Colporteur Ministry
COL	Christ's Object Lessons
Con	Confrontation
COS	Christ Our Saviour
CS	Counsels on Stewardship
CSW	Counsels on Sabbath School Work
CT	Counsels to Parents, Teachers, and Students
CTBH	Christian Temperance (EGW) and Bible Hygiene (James White)
CTr	Christ Triumphant
CW	Counsels to Writers and Editors
DA	Desire of Ages, The
DF	Document File
DG	Daughters of God
Ed	Education
Ev	Evangelism
EW	Early Writings
FE	Fundamentals of Christian Education
FLB	Faith I Live By, The

FH	From the Heart
FW	Faith and Works
GC	Great Controversy, The
GC88	Great Controversy, The (1888 Edition)
GCB	General Conference Bulletin
GCDB	General Conference Daily Bulletin
GdH	Good Health
GH	Gospel Herald
GW	Gospel Workers
GW92	Gospel Workers (1892 edition)
HL	Healthful Living
HP	In Heavenly Places
HPMMW	Health, Philanthropic, and Medical Missionary Work
HR	Health Reformer
HS	Historical Sketches of the Foreign Missions of the Seventh-day Adventists
Hvn	Heaven
LDE	Last Day Events
LHU	Lift Him Up
LL	Lion on the Loose
LP	Sketches From the Life of Paul
LS	Life Sketches of Ellen G. White
LS88	Life Sketches of James and Ellen White (1888 edition)
Lt	Letter, E. G. White
LYL	Letters to Young Lovers
Mar	Maranatha, the Lord is Coming
MB	Thoughts From the Mount of Blessing
1MCP	Mind, Character and Personality, Vol. 1 (2MCP for Vol. 2)
MH	Ministry of Healing, The
ML	My Life Today
MM	Medical Ministry
1MR	Manuscript Releases, Vol. 1 (2MR for Vol. 2, etc.)
Ms	Manuscript, E. G. White
MYP	Messages to Young People
NL	New Life, A
1NL	Notebook Leaflets, Vol. 1 (2NL for Vol. 2)
PaM	Pastoral Ministry
OFC	Our Father Cares
OHC	Our High Calling
PHJ	Pacific Health Journal
PM	Publishing Ministry, The
PP	Patriarchs and Prophets
PK	Prophets and Kings
Pr	Prayer
PUR	Pacific Union Recorder
RC	Reflecting Christ

RH	Review and Herald
RR	Radiant Religion
RY	Retirement Years, The
SA	Solemn Appeal, A
1SAT	Sermons and Talks, Vol. 1 (2SAT for Vol. 2)
SC	Steps to Christ
SD	Sons and Daughters of God
SF Echo	Southern Field Echo
1SG	Spiritual Gifts, Vols. 1 (3SG for Vols. 3, etc.)
SJ	Steps to Jesus (adapted from SC) or Story of Jesus (on CD-ROM)
SL	Sanctified Life, The
1SM	Selected Messages, Book One (2SM for Book 2, etc.)
SOJ	Story of Jesus, The
1SP	Spirit of Prophecy, The, Vol. 1 (2SP for Vol. 2, etc.)
SpT"A"	Special Testimonies, Series A (Nos. 1-12)
SpT"B"	Special Testimonies, Series B (Nos. 1-19)
SpTBCC	Special Testimonies to the Battle Creek Church
SpTEd	Special Testimonies on Education
SpTMMW	Special Testimonies Relating to Medical Missionary Work
SpTMWI	Special Testimonies to Managers and Workers in Institutions
SpTPH	Special Testimonies to Physicians and Helpers
SR	Story of Redemption, The
ST	Signs of the Times
SW	Southern Work, The
SW	Southern Watchman (if with date)
1T	Testimonies for the Church Vol. 1 (2T for Vol. 2, etc.)
TA	Truth About Angels, The
TDG	This Day With God
Te	Temperance
TM	Testimonies to Ministers and Gospel Workers
TMK	That I May Know Him
TSA	Testimonies to Southern Africa
TSB	Testimonies on Sexual Behaviour, Adultery, and Divorce
TSDF	Testimony Studies on Diet and Foods
TSS	Selections From the Testimonies Bearing on Sabbath School Work (1900)
1TT	Testimony Treasures, Vol. 1 (2TT for Vol. 2, etc.)
UL	Upward Look, The
Und Ms	Undated EGW Manuscript
VSS	Voice in Speech and Song, The
WM	Welfare Ministry
YI	Youth's Instructor, The
YRP	Ye Shall Receive Power, A
WLF	Word to the "Little Flock," A

Made in the USA
San Bernardino, CA
16 April 2018